Proofreading/Editing Proficiency

a text-workbook

Y0-CDR-726

Judith C. Simon, Ed.D.

Memphis State University

Glencoe Publishing Company
Encino, California

Copyright © 1986 by Glencoe Publishing Company, a division of Macmillan, Inc.

All rights reserved. No part of this book shall be reproduced or transmitted in any form or by any means, electronic or mechanical, including photocopying, recording, or by any information retrieval system, without written permission from the Publisher.

Send all inquiries to:
Glencoe Publishing Company
17337 Ventura Boulevard
Encino, California 91316

Printed in the United States of America

Library of Congress Cataloging-in-Publication Data

Simon, Judith C.

Proofreading/editing proficiency.

1. Copy-reading—Handbooks, manuals, etc.   2. Proofreading—Handbooks, manuals, etc.   3. Copyreading—Problems, exercises, etc.   4. Proofreading—Problems, exercises, etc.   I. Title.
PN162.S53   1986   070.4′15   85-17581
ISBN 0-02-683060-4
ISBN 0-02-683070-1 (Instructor's Guide)
1 2 3 4 5 6 7 8 9   91 90 89 88 87 86

CONTENTS

Acknowledgments

Gratitude is expressed to all those who have helped with this project. Special thanks go to Dr. Lillian Greathouse and Dr. Patricia Merrier for their helpful comments and suggestions during the development of the book, to Dennis Gladhill and John Gastineau for their editorial assistance, and to Glynda Luttman for her typewriting skills.

Preface

Good proofreading and editing skills are necessary to produce the clear, accurate written messages that make businesses operate efficiently and effectively. This text is designed to give students instruction and realistic experience to master those skills.

Proofreading/Editing Proficiency was written with three basic ideas in mind:

1. Proofreading and editing are interrelated activities, both involving careful reading of material for accuracy of information and for clarity of content.
2. The principles of clear, effective written communication are the same whether a document is prepared by hand or by a word processor.
3. Students cannot master proofreading and editing skills without clear explanation of the principles of written communications, without examples of how those principles are employed, or without extensive practice in the use of those principles.

Proofreading/Editing Proficiency combines coverage of both activities in one volume but emphasizes proofreading because it is the skill that will be most frequently used by the student on the job. Editing concerns that can be addressed independently of proofreading are highlighted by sections called *Pencil Points*.

The text recognizes that modern office equipment and software can present technical problems in the production of documents. However, because the principles of good writing are the same no matter how a document is produced, it suggests adaptation of traditional techniques as the most effective means of coping with those problems rather than creating new and unnecessarily complicated systems.

Appropriate for students at both the secondary and postsecondary levels who are training for work in business offices, the text may be used in a variety of courses, including typewriting, word processing, office procedures, and business communication. It is also appropriate for use in training sessions for employees in businesses.

The chapters are written in a concise, easy-to-read manner. They can be studied on an individual, self-paced basis or can be presented in a teacher-directed environment.

Proficiency in editing and proofreading is developed through the use of realistic practice materials. Each chapter of this text contains ten exercises related to the contents of that chapter and designed to develop both proofreading and editing skills. The exercises are placed at the end of the chapter so that they can be removed after completion without affecting the chapter contents. The book can then be retained for use as a reference manual.

The exercises in each chapter proceed from simple to complex. The first exercises are directed toward specific chapter principles; the final exercises combine a variety of concepts.

To provide realism, the exercises do not contain a set number of errors. The number of errors varies in each exercise to force students to read as carefully as would be needed in an actual office job. The exercises reflect realistic business documents and situations and provide practice in proofreading documents produced in an electronic office. The student is given the opportunity to practice proofreading graphic materials such as tables, pie charts, and bar graphs, and to use and interpret standard revision marks.

The final section of the book contains an ''in-basket'' simulation involving 20 exercises. This project provides an opportunity for students to practice using the proofreading and editing concepts in a specific, more businesslike setting, with business forms used where appropriate. Students are not told what types of errors are contained in each exercise. Some of the exercises contain related information, and students are expected to check the consistency of information from one document to another.

The Instructor's Guide includes tests for use with each of the 12 chapters, answers to all exercises, suggested teaching and evaluation methods, and a bibliography of additional sources of information.

Chapter

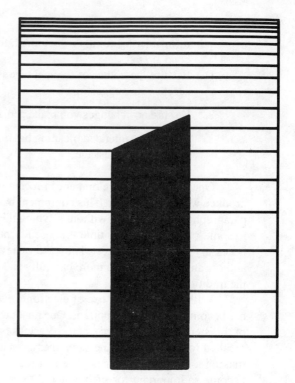

PROOFREADING/ EDITING SKILL DEVELOPMENT TECHNIQUES

❓ What's Wrong Here?

Seen on a sports page: He was their first player to run for 1,000 years.

Proofreading and editing skills can be improved through study and practice using appropriate techniques. The materials in this text are designed to give you the opportunity to practice using those techniques so that you can develop good proofreading and editing skills.

Remember that just learning the principles of good writing and completing the practice exercises will not ensure that you will have good proofreading and editing skills. You must make a conscious effort to continually apply these skills to the different types of work you do elsewhere. You must *want* to find errors before you can proofread and edit successfully.

Since the invention of the typewriter, proofreading has primarily involved the search for errors in spelling and typewriting. Today, a good proofreader is sometimes expected to make additional changes or "edit" the material to improve its content. Editing includes being able to find and correct errors in grammar, punctuation, capitalization, expression of numbers, abbreviations, hyphenation, word usage, and format.

Proofreading involves checking the accuracy of materials. Every written item to be used in the operation of a business must be checked carefully for accuracy of information. Some information is proofread several times—after initial typing, after revisions are made, and after final typing. Little variation exists concerning the amount of proofreading expected; *every* written document must be proofread before being sent to its destination.

Editing is the process of making changes to improve a written message. The meaning of any written message must be clear to the receiver of the message. The words used must be understandable, and they must be correctly placed within the sentences. In addition, sentences must be properly punctuated to provide clear meanings. Office employees are expected to recognize and correct basic errors in sentence wording and punctuation. The amount of editing expected varies from one office situation to another, but office employees who are promoted to higher levels have usually demonstrated that they possess good editing skills.

When considering editing a document, follow these guides:

1. Be sure the author of the message is willing to let you make changes and is likely to accept your suggestions.

2. Be sure any changes you make actually improve the document.

3. Be sure the intended meaning has not been altered. When you are not sure, consult the author of the message.

One significant development in recent years has been the use of electronic equipment to produce written messages. This equipment has made revision much easier. For example, whole paragraphs can be moved without retyping them; and in one simple step, a term can be changed to some other word every time it is used throughout many pages of text. Very little retyping is necessary to make changes. The ease of revision with electronic equipment has encouraged authors and typists to read more carefully and to make far more changes than were feasible with the traditional typewriter.

With the increasing use of electronic equipment, careful checking of business documents has become even more important. One major reason for using such equipment is to take advantage of the memory or storage capacity. Various paragraphs and entire messages are stored and later recalled for further use. The same messages are frequently sent to many destinations by simply making a few name changes. The fact that one message is used repeatedly explains why it has become so important for such material to be correct. An error in a sentence being used in form letters sent to thousands of customers would be very serious. Of course, an error in any message should be considered serious, regardless of the number of copies sent.

The use of electronic equipment such as word processors and microcomputers has eased the task of correcting documents. However, the biggest difficulty has always been that of *finding* the areas needing change. Locating needed changes is still a very important job, regardless of the equipment being used to produce the message.

The terms *proofreading* and *editing* are sometimes used interchangeably today because the procedures involved are quite similar; both activities may be performed during one review of a document. The primary emphasis in this text is on proofreading, but some important editing concepts are included. We call these concepts ''pencil points,'' and they will be indicated by the illustration you see at the beginning of this paragraph. ■

■ IMPORTANCE OF PROOFREADING AND EDITING SKILLS

Employees of business organizations produce many documents daily. Accuracy is considered extremely important; one small error could conceivably cause very serious problems.

Accurate, clearly stated, and attractively presented written documents have these effects:

1. increased efficiency due to a decreased need for later explanations or corrections,

2. increased employee pride in the business,

3. indication that business employees know what they are doing,

4. indication that the author places importance on the receiver of the message,

5. improvement in the overall image of the company to those outside the organization.

■ Typical Proofreading Errors

One way to improve your proofreading skills is to be aware of the most common types of proofreading errors and the locations where these errors often occur. Extra attention to these areas can help you develop good proofreading skills.

The most common types of proofreading errors, according to research, are:

1. Transposition of words within sentences

    It is hoped this that will become an annual event.
    > instead of

    It is hoped that this will become an annual event.

2. Substitution of one small word for another

    We are sure it in the best product available.
    > instead of

    We are sure it is the best product available.

3. Omission of one doubled letter

    We are especialy proud of our service.
    > instead of

    We are especially proud of our service.

4. Omission of a letter within a word

    This is an exampe of a typical error.
    > instead of

    This is an example of a typical error.

5. Doubling of small words or of syllables within a word

    New forms will be be available tomorrow.
    > instead of

    New forms will be available tomorrow.

    Please rememember to call me Friday.
    > instead of

    Please remember to call me Friday.

6. Transposition of letters within a word

    Please send us your quailfications.
    > instead of

    Please send us your qualifications.

7. Omission of an entire word in a sentence

    It will be possible for me to attend.
    > instead of

    It will not be possible for me to attend.

Studies have also determined locations where proofreading errors often occur. These locations are listed and illustrated below. The numbers in the illustration correspond with the location numbers listed on the left side of the page.

Locations where proofreading errors often occur:

1. in proper nouns

2. in headings or subheadings

3. in vertical enumerations

4. near the beginning or the end of lines

5. in long words that occur rather frequently

6. in number combinations

7. near the bottom of the page

```
January 12, 19--


Mr. Alvin Edwards
Personnel Director
Federated Industries
Tulsa, OK  74125
                      ①
Dear Mr. Edward:        ②

      SUBJECT:  You Order for Three Mahogany Desks

Thank you for your order for three mahogany desks.
You made afine choice in office furniture.

Before your desks can be sent, we need the following
additional information:

1.  exact size of desk desired, 30" X 54" or 36" X 60"

2.  the specific locations were you would like the
    desks delivered   ③

3.  the method of payment (20 percent downpayment is
    required)
④
Simple complete and return the enclosed card to give
us the ⑤neccessary information.  As soon as we receive
the card and you ⑥25 percent downpayment, we will
complete your order and deliver your desks.

Sincerly,  ⑦


Joseph P. Smith
Shipping


pc


Enclosure
```

RELATED ASSIGNMENT:	EXERCISE 1.1,	PAGE 11
	EXERCISE 1.2,	PAGE 12
	EXERCISE 1.3,	PAGE 13

■ METHODS OF PROOFREADING AND EDITING

Several methods for finding errors are effective. Here are some specific suggestions to help you:

1. Take your time. Make a special effort to read *slowly*.

2. Read the material twice, once for spelling and typographical errors and once for content. To read *very* carefully for spelling and typographical errors, try reading the material from right to left rather than left to right. Reading aloud usually helps, too.

3. If you are checking material you have typed, read the material *before* removing the page from the machine. Roll the paper back so you are at the top of the page; slowly roll the paper forward, using the paper bail to guide you to check only one line at a time.

4. When checking material that is not in a machine, turn the paper to a different angle or place some brightly colored material under it to get a different view. The change in appearance of the page makes errors easier to locate.

5. When accuracy is *extremely* important, use the cooperative method—one person checking the final copy while another reads aloud. This method is not practical for *all* proofreading because it requires the time of two workers. One well-trained proofreader should be able to locate and correct most errors under normal circumstances.

6. Verify the accuracy of any mathematical calculations (recalculate them).

7. When in doubt about the accuracy of the material you are checking, consult a dictionary, a style manual, or another appropriate reference book.

8. When you are checking material on a video display screen, several methods are possible:
   a. Use a plastic ruler or sheet of paper to block from view all lines below the line you are reading. Locating errors is easier when you have only a small area in view rather than an entire page.
   b. Use the cursor and move slowly across each line; using the cursor helps you to read slowly and tells you exactly how far you have read.
   c. Use the cursor or other line-guide features to move down the page one line at a time.

It is usually more efficient to check the material on the screen rather than to print a copy first. When you are proofreading material on the screen, you can make any needed changes as soon as you locate errors. When you proofread a printed copy, it takes more time to make corrections because you must still view the material on the screen and locate the errors before changes can be made. It is considered more efficient to proofread from a paper copy in instances in which part of the horizontal line used for the message is not visible on the screen. In addition, proofreading may be more effective on a printed copy when glare or contrast causes difficulty in reading material on the screen.

■ REVISION MARKS

Revision marks are usually used as a method of indicating specific changes to be made to written materials. Revision marks are fairly standardized and are used as an efficient means of clearly communicating needed changes.

Sometimes the author of a message will read a typical draft and will then use revision marks to indicate desired changes. When the material is returned for final typing, the typist must understand these marks to be able to interpret the requests for change.

Additional marks or instructions are often placed in margins. These marginal comments are used to clear up any confusion that may occur among an author, an operator, and a proofreader. Any mark or instruction that can be easily understood is acceptable.

Revision marks for insertions, deletions, replacements, and moves are widely used in word processing operations. Marginal notes are often added to materials to indicate *global* changes. Global changes are those that affect the entire document. For example, a revision mark might instruct the word processing employee to delete the word *writer* and insert the word *author*. An additional note or mark indicating that this is a global change would mean that *every* reference to *writer* should be changed to *author*. Specific symbols for global changes have not become uniform enough to be considered standard. Methods being used to indicate global changes include:

1. writing the word *global* in the margin or near the revision.
2. writing *GL* in the margin or near the revision.
3. placing a circle around the revision.

Some of the most widely used revision marks are shown at the end of this section. Exercises are provided at the end of each chapter for you to develop your proofreading and editing skills. You will have an opportunity to use revision marks in most of the exercises. Since the exercises are located at the end of each chapter, the chapter contents can be kept intact for use as a reference manual after the exercises have been completed and removed.

STANDARD REVISION MARKS

Format/Appearance Revisions

Mark	Meaning	Draft Copy	Revision
SS	*single-space*	Your reports are SS due Friday.	Your reports are due Friday.
ds	*double-space*	ds Keep up the good work.	Keep up the good work.
ts	*triple-space*	ts The meeting is on Friday.	The meeting is on Friday.
#	*insert space*	It will take sometime to finish.	It will take some time to finish.
◡	*close up space*	Please come some time this week.	Please come sometime this week.

Mark	Meaning	Draft Copy	Revision
‖	*align vertically*	2.01 ‖ 3.06 ‖ .24 ‖	2.01 3.06 .24
=	*align horizontally*	Contact Joe‗ if you have questions.	Contact Joe if you have questions.
₵	*new paragraph*	₵ Please call if we can help.	Please call if we can help.
5⌐	*indent 5 spaces*	5⌐Your materials are enclosed.	Your materials are enclosed.
cap or ‗	*use capital letters*	John drove mr.‗ cap davis home.	John drove Mr. Davis home.
lc or /	*use lowercase letters*	We toured two /Plants last lc Week.	We toured two plants last week.
O	*spell out*	We need to finish ②reports.	We need to finish two reports.
[	*move to left*	[Your report was received today.	Your report was received today.
]	*move to right*	Miami] Tampa Bay	Miami Tampa Bay
] [	*center horizontally*	] Miami [Tampa Bay	Miami Tampa Bay
∿	*boldface print*	Proofreading ∿∿∿ is an important activity.	**Proofreading** is an important activity.

Content Revisions

Mark	Meaning	Draft Copy	Revision
∧	*insert information*	Martin went ^{to}∧ the meeting.	Martin went to the meeting.
ℓ / or ___	*delete information*	Dave spoke t̶o̶ to the ~~the~~ participants.	Dave spoke to the participants.
⌄	*insert comma*	Our new office is in Euless∧ Texas.	Our new office is in Euless, Texas.
⌄	*insert semicolon*	We're closed Friday∧we reopen Monday.	We're closed Friday; we reopen Monday.
⌄	*insert colon*	Please buy the following∧pens, pencils, paper.	Please buy the following: pens, pencils, paper.
⌄	*insert apostrophe*	Don⌄t be late to the meeting.	Don't be late to the meeting.
⌄	*insert quotation marks*	The word ⌄eager⌄ describes our staff.	The word "eager" describes our staff.
⊙	*change to or insert a period*	Dr⊙ Jo Isaki will arrive today.	Dr. Jo Isaki will arrive today.

Mark	Meaning	Draft Copy	Revision
=/	*insert hyphen*	=/ Your last minute ∧ change was approved.	Your last-minute change was approved.
--/	*insert dash*	--/ We are always busy especially ∧ on Fridays.	We are always busy--especially on Fridays.
(/)	*insert parentheses*	(/) The percent symbol % is used in tables.	The percent symbol (%) is used in tables.
⌇	*delete letter and close up space*	We will call you latⁱer this month.	We will call you later this month.
∽	*transpose*	We will able be to increase our benefits soon.	We will be able to increase our benefits soon.
O→	*move*	On April 2 Jackson drove 300 miles.	Jackson drove 300 miles on April 2.
• • •	*ignore revision*	Call Gregg before Thursday's meeting.	Call Gregg before Thursday's meeting.

END-OF-CHAPTER ASSIGNMENT:	**EXERCISES 1.4 THROUGH 1.10, PAGES 14 THROUGH 20.**

▤ EXERCISE

Use the list of common types of proofreading errors as a guide to help you locate the errors in the sentences below. Write the corrected sentence in the blank space below each sentence or use revision marks to indicate corrections.

I hope I can go to to the meeting today.

I am going no a short trip next week.

I will go to the review session it if doesn't conflict with my schedule.

It in getting close to the deadline for submitting new ideas.

The final agenda is due the later part of next week.

In September I am going visit our branch office in Jackson.

We have plants in all parts of the word.

We will being typing our reports on work processing equipment next week.

I hope the employee donations to the fund will accumumulate quickly.

The attachment came lose from the letter.

▤ EXERCISE

Use the list of common types of proofreading errors as a guide to help you test your proofreading skill. Compare the original copy of the paragraph below with the final copy. Use revision marks to indicate changes needed in the final copy.

Original Copy

> Many problems can be caused by a typist's inability to proofread accurately. Any error that is undetected by the typist could cause an individual or a business a great deal of embarrassment as well as possible financial loss.

Final Copy

Many problems can be caused by a typist's inability to to profread accurately.   Any error that is undetected by the typist could cuase an individual of a business a great deal of embarassment is well as possible finanancial loss.

📋 EXERCISE 1.3

Use the list of locations where proofreading errors often occur as an aid in locating errors in this letter. Compare the original copy with the final copy. Use revision marks to indicate changes needed on the final copy.

Original Copy	**Final Copy**
December 21, 19--	December 21,19--
Mrs. Jerry Johnson 1222 Longview College Station, TX 77841	Mrs. Jerry Johnson 1222 Longview College Station, TX 77481
Dear Mrs. Johnson:	Dear Mrs. Johnson:
Subject: Your New Account	Subject: You New Account
Congratulations! You are the recipient of a new charge account card for use at our store. Here are some of its benefits:	Congradulations! You are the recipient of a new charge account card for use at our store. Here are some of its benefits:
1. You can carry a balance in your account up to $500.	1. You can carry a balance in your account up to $50.
2. You need pay only $10 per month.	2. You need pay only $10 per month.
3. You only write us one check per month rather than writing a check for each purchase.	3. You olny write us one check per month rather than writing a check for each purchase.
Remember, our annual half-price sale begins next week. We look forward to seeing you then.	Rememember, our annual half- price sale begins next week. We look forward to seeing you then.
Sincerely yours,	Sincerely yours,
Maurice Katz Credit Department	Mourice Katz Credit Department
lj	lj
Enclosure	Enclosure

目 EXERCISE 1.4

Complete the exercise below to practice proofreading frequently used words. Compare the words on the left with those on the right. Use revision marks to change any item in the column on the right that is not identical to the corresponding item on the left.

Original Copy	Final Copy
than	then
percent	percent
amount	amount
necessary	necessary
remember	rememember
through	thorough
payment	payments
forward	forward
possibly	possible
department	department
accumulate	accummulate
analyze	analyze
already	already
anxious	anxious
similar	similiar
among	amoung
confident	confidence
usually	usually
cannot	cannot
convenience	convenient

📋 EXERCISE

Complete the exercise below to practice proofreading number combinations. Compare the figures on the left with those on the right. Assume that the figures on the left are correct. Use revision marks to change any item in the column on the right that is not identical to the corresponding item on the left.

Original Copy	Final Copy
$777,888.21	$777,888.12
665,321.14	65,321.14
371,737.37	371,237.37
8,827.40	8,827.40
651,372.00	657,312.00
1,355.04	1,533.04
752,365.99	152,365.99
66,424.00	99,424.00
37,514.92	37,514.92
83,833.38	83,883.38
66,341.11	66,341.00
1,411.77	1,411.77
327.49	327.49
942,000.47	992,000.47
64,271.01	64,277.01
32,584.61	32,584.61
41,761.07	47,161.07
23,509.76	32,509,76
1,446.83	1,446.83
141,835.92	141,835.92
65,221.84	56,221.84
71,340.00	71,340.00
29,856.63	29,856.63
44,221.15	44,221.15
711,356.29	771,356.29

📋 EXERCISE 1.6

Complete the exercise below to practice proofreading frequently used long words. (Some of these words will appear again in the spelling practice.) Compare the words on the left with the words on the right. Use revision marks to change any item in the column on the right that is not identical to the corresponding item on the left. Assume that the words in the original copy are correct.

Original Copy	Final Copy
congratulations	congratulations
interchangeable	interchangable
accompanying	accompaning
occasionally	occassionally
especially	expecially
correspondence	correspondence
knowledgeable	knowledgeable
miscellaneous	miscellaneous
questionnaire	questionaire
interpretation	interpretation
absenteeism	absenteeeism
acknowledgment	acknowledgment
automatically	automaticaly
clarification	clarifification
compensation	compensation
consecutive	consecutive
coordinator	coordination
denomination	denominator
documentation	documentation
hospitalization	hospitlization

📄 EXERCISE 1.7

Complete this exercise to practice proofreading proper nouns. Compare the proper nouns on the left with the ones on the right. Use revision marks to change any item in the column on the right that is not identical to the corresponding item on the left. Assume that the proper nouns on the left are correct.

Original Copy	Final Copy
Tuscaloosa, Alabama	Tucsaloosa, Alabama
Mount Rushmore	Mount Rushmore
Canfield Clinic	Camfield Clinic
Monday, July 4	Monday, July 4
Ferdinando Hernandez	Ferdinand Hernandez
Schenectady, New York	Schenectady, New York
Broken Arrow, Oklahoma	Broken Bow, Oklahoma
Taft-Hartley Act	Taft-Hartly Act
Tennessee Valley Authority	Tennessee Valley Authority
Dogwood Villa Lane	Dogwood Ville Lane
United States Postal Service	United States Postal Service
Mathematics 1203	Mathmatics 1203
Who's Who in America	Who's Who in America
Department of the Interior	Department of Interior
First National Bank	First National Bank
Pablo Picasso	Pablo Picasso
Mediterranean Sea	Mediterrannean Sea
West Texas State University	West Texas State University
American Medical Association	American Medicine Association
King Constantine	Kind Constantine

📋 EXERCISE 1.8

Complete the exercise below to practice proofreading vertical enumerations (as well as proper nouns). Compare the cities on the left with those on the right. Assume that the original copy is correct. Use revision marks to change any item in the column on the right that is not identical to the corresponding item on the left.

Original Copy

We will be driving across the country in July.   Listed below are some of the places we plan to visit:

1.   Albuquerque, NM 87114
2.   Charleston, SC 29407
3.   Chattanooga, TN 37419
4.   Chickasha, OK 73018
5.   Durham, NC 27703
6.   El Cajon, CA 92021
7.   Flagstaff, AZ 86001
8.   Greenville, SC 29611
9.   Grenada, MS 38901
10.   Hot Springs, AR 71909
11.   Jackson, MS 39212
12.   Knoxville, TN 37921
13.   Las Vegas, NV 89117
14.   Little Rock, AR 72207
15.   Norman, OK 73069
16.   Pasadena, CA 91102
17.   Raleigh, NC 27602
18.   Reno, NV 89510

Final Copy

We will be driving across the country in July.   Listed below are some of the places we plan to visit:

1.   Albuquerque, NM 78114
2.   Charleston, SC 29407
3.   Chattanooqa, TN 37419
4.   Chichasha, OK 73018
5.   Durham, NC 27703
6.   El Cajon, AC 92021
7.   Flagstaff, AR 86001
8.   Greenville, SC 29611
9.   Grenada, MI 38901
10.   Hot Springs, AR
11.   Jackson, MS 39212
12.   Knoxville, TN 37921
13.   Las Vegas, NV 89117
14.   Little Rock, AR 73207
15.   Norman, OK
16.   Psaadena, CA 911102
17.   Raleigh, NC 47602
18.   Reno, NV 89510

▤ EXERCISE

Complete the exercise below to practice proofreading a combination of proper nouns and number combinations. Compare the names and addresses on the left with those on the right. Assume that the original copy is correct. Use revision marks to change any item in the column on the right that is not identical to the corresponding item on the left.

Original Copy

Mr. Walter Stribling
8645 Melrose Lane
Seattle, Washington 98122

Mr. Clifford Canfield
2101 Biggers Boulevard
Aberdeen, South Dakota 41990

Mrs. George Jackson
1449 Riverside Drive
Covington, Kentucky 41010

Dr. Frederick Jones
3149 Harrison Street
Aaronsburg, Pennsylvania 15926

Mrs. Marshall Smithee
5522 Beech Lane
Albuquerque, Mew Mexico 87104

Mr. Edward Benson
7820 East 22nd Drive
Tulsa, Oklahoma 74129

Mr. David Milburn
1919 Evergreen
Cincinnati, Ohio 45240

Mrs. William Carnes
100 Stanford
Tyler, Texas 75701

Mr. Howard Graham
128 East 26th
Kalamazoo, Michigan 49002

Mrs. Terry Chamberlain
92751 Holly Avenue
San Jose, California 91520

Final Copy

Mr. Walter Stribling
8645 Melrose Lane
Seattle, Washington 99122

Mr. Clifford Canfield
2011 Biggers Boulevard
Aberdeen, South Dakota 41990

Mrs. George Jackson
1449 Riverside Drive
Covington, Kentucky 41019

Mr. Frederick Jones
3144 Harrison Street
Aaronsburg, Pennsylvania 15926

Mrs. Marshall Smithe
5522 Beach Lane
Albuquerque, Mew Mexico 87104

Mr. Edward Benson
7824 East 32nd Drive
Tulsa, Oklahoma 74129

Mr. David Milbern
1919 Evergreen
Cincinnati, Ohio 45240

Mrs. William Carnes
100 Stamford
Tyler, Texas 75701

Mr. Howard Graham
128 East 26th
Kalamazoo, Mickigan 49002

Mrs. Terry Chamberland
92751 Holly Avenue
San Jose, California 91520

📖 EXERCISE

Complete the exercise below to practice proofreading material in a letter format with a variety of errors included. Compare the letter on the left with the one on the right. Use revision marks to change any item in the letter on the right that is not identical to the material on the left.

Original Copy

March 14, 19--

Mr. A. A. Allen
445 Davis Drive
Billings, MT 59102

Dear Mr. Allen:

We wrote you last month about the delinquency of payments on your loan. We have received neither a reply nor your payment. Two installments, amounting to $548, are now due.

Can you make a substantial payment on your account within ten days? If not, we shall have to ask the trustees to begin proceedings in accordance with the terms of your deed. The expense of this action will be chargeable to you.

We sincerely hope you will give this account your prompt attention and avoid the expense and inconvenience of the action mentioned above.

Sincerely yours,

F. L. Bailey
Secretary

Final Copy

March 24, 19--

Mr. A. A. Allan
445 Davis Drive
Billings, MI 59102

Dear Mr. Allen:

We wrote you last month about the delinquency of payments on you loan. We have received neither a reply or your payment. Two installments, amounting to $548, are not due.

Can you make a substantial payment on your account within ten days? If not, we shall have to ask the trustees to begin proceedings in accordance with the terms of the deed. The expense of this action will be chargeable to us.

We sincerely hope you will give this account your prompt attention amd avoid the expense and inconvenience of the action mentioned above.

Sincerely yours,

E. L. Bailey
Secretary

<h1>Chapter</h1>

<h1>GRAMMAR REVIEW</h1>

What's Wrong Here?

Seen in a report: Typing rapidly, the letter was finished by the deadline.

All written messages must be grammatically correct. Messages with incorrect grammar can cause misunderstandings and will certainly leave a bad impression on anyone who sees them.

■ TECHNIQUES FOR IMPROVING GRAMMAR

Many aids are available for checking grammatical usage. Dictionaries list the ways in which words are used as a part of their descriptions (noun, verb, etc.). This information can help you determine if a word is being used appropriately in a specific sentence.

Example: Look up the word *accurate* in a dictionary. In addition to its pronunciation, you will see that it is used as an adjective. Definitions are also given, such as "free from error." Other forms of the word are given, such as *accurately*. Parts of speech for these words are also given: *accurately* is an adverb.

Words are listed alphabetically in the dictionary, with the preferred spelling shown first. Each entry also includes:

1. separation of word into individual syllables

2. pronunciation

3. part(s) of speech

4. definition(s)

Many other reference books are available, such as:

1. word books, which list frequently used words and acceptable locations for word division.

2. office handbooks, which provide examples of letter styles and list rules for grammar, punctuation, etc., along with other guides for working efficiently.

3. report style manuals, which give detailed directions and examples for typing formal reports.

Dictionaries and other good reference books should be kept near your working area so they can be consulted when you are in doubt about the correctness of a message.

In addition to having reference materials available, you can improve your chances of finding and correcting errors by reviewing grammar rules. If you know the rules of grammar, you are more likely to recognize errors.

Grammatical areas that cause the most difficulty are reviewed in the remaining sections of this chapter. In addition, related exercises are provided to help you practice locating and correcting grammatical errors as you proofread various types of material.

■ TENSE

Tense is related to expression of time. Keep these guidelines in mind for using the appropriate tense:

1. Use past tense to describe something that has already occurred and is finished.

    Past tense: The employee performance evaluations <u>were</u> <u>completed</u> yesterday.

2. Use present tense to describe something that exists or is true now, even if it was also true in the past.

    Present tense: Most employees <u>are</u> <u>happy</u> with the results of their evaluations.

3. Use future tense to describe something that has not occurred.

    Future tense: The next employee evaluations <u>will</u> be <u>completed</u> in six months.

4. Avoid switching back and forth from one tense to another.

    Incorrect tense: <u>Last</u> week, I <u>ask</u> for a salary increase.
    (past tense and present tense)

    Correct tense: <u>Last</u> week, I <u>asked</u> for a salary increase.
    (past tense and past tense)

■ SENTENCE CONSTRUCTION

Business messages should be written in complete sentences. Incomplete sentences are called *sentence fragments* and are used mainly to attract unusual attention. They are not considered appropriate for most business situations. Sentence fragments are acceptable only in very informal writing or in advertising messages where they are used for emphasis.

A complete sentence must contain a complete thought and must include both a *subject* and a *predicate* (or *verb*).

Subject: the person, place, or thing that the sentence is about (usually a noun or a pronoun).

Predicate: what is said about the subject (mainly a verb and modifiers); the word *verb* is often used today for the predicate.

Complete sentence:	John wrote the report.
	(Subject = John; verb = wrote)
Incomplete sentence:	While John wrote the report.
	(Contains a noun and a verb but is an incomplete thought)

If you are preparing materials for someone else and are unsure of the intended meaning of a sentence, take the time to consult the author of the message. You will want to be sure that any changes you make improve the writing without changing the meaning of sentences. ∎

| RELATED ASSIGNMENT: | EXERCISE 2.1, | PAGE 29 |
| | EXERCISE 2.2, | PAGE 30 |

■ SUBJECT/VERB AGREEMENT

Since the verb or predicate is what is said about the subject, the verb must agree with its subject in number. Here are some guidelines to help you with subject/verb agreement:

1. A singular subject must have a singular verb; a plural subject must have a plural verb.

    Three boxes of supplies are being shipped today.
    (plural subject; plural verb)

    One box of supplies is being shipped today.
    (singular subject; singular verb)

Note: An exception to this rule relates to the pronoun *you:* when *you* is the subject of a sentence, a plural verb is *always* used, even if the reference is to a singular subject.

    You are expected to be on time.
    (You as subject; plural verb)

2. When two or more singular subjects are included in a sentence and are joined by *and,* a plural verb is usually required because a plural subject has been created.

    Lillian and Patricia are going to the meeting.
    (two subjects; plural verb)

3. When two or more singular subjects are included in a sentence and are joined by *or* or *nor*, a singular verb is usually required because only one of the subjects is involved in the action of the verb.

    Either a memo or a letter is an acceptable format for this message to employees.
    (singular subject; singular verb)

4. When both singular and plural subjects are included in a sentence and are joined by *or* or *nor,* the verb should agree with the subject nearest the verb.

    Neither Joe nor his assistants are planning to attend the regional meeting.
    (subject closest to verb is plural; plural verb)

    Either the workers or a supervisor is available to answer questions.
    (subject closest to verb is singular; singular verb)

5. When *each* or *every* precedes the parts joined by *and* in a compound subject, the verb is singular.

> Each man and woman in the office is eligible for the award.

> Every man and woman in the office is involved in the new program.

6. Indefinite pronouns, such as *someone, everybody,* and *no one,* are considered singular and require a singular verb.

> No one who arrived Thursday is leaving the conference before Saturday.

> Everyone who wants to participate is meeting at 4 p.m.

7. A collective noun refers to a group of persons or objects. When a collective noun refers to a group as a whole or as a unit, a singular verb is used; when the reference is to individuals within the group, a plural verb is used.

> The committee is in favor of the change in plans.
> (one unit)

> A number of workers were absent yesterday.
> (reference to individuals)

8. The verb must agree with the subject in number even when there are modifiers of a different number. (*Modifier:* words or groups of words that describe, limit, or make more exact the meaning of other words.)

> **Incorrect verb choice:** The final report, including six appendix sections, are being mailed today.

> **Correct verb choice:** The final report, including six appendix sections, is being mailed today.

RELATED ASSIGNMENT:	EXERCISE 2.3, PAGE 31
	EXERCISE 2.4, PAGE 32

■ PRONOUN/ANTECEDENT AGREEMENT

A pronoun is a word used in place of a noun. We often use pronouns to avoid repeating words and to add variety and clarity to our messages. The pronoun used must be correctly chosen based on its antecedent (*antecedent:* the word, phrase, or clause to which the pronoun refers). The antecedent can be singular or plural and can also be masculine, feminine, or neuter in gender. The pronoun and its antecedent must agree in person, number, and gender.

The guidelines for pronoun/antecedent agreement are similar to those for subject/verb agreement. Here are some important ones to remember:

1. Use a singular pronoun to refer to a singular antecedent and a plural pronoun to refer to a plural antecedent.

> The supervisor left her notes in the conference room.
> (singular pronoun for singular antecedent)

> All the employees completed their reports on time.
> (plural pronoun for plural antecedent)

2. Use a singular pronoun when a collective noun stands for a group considered as a unit and a plural pronoun when a collective noun stands for the individuals in the group considered separately.

> Our company basketball <u>team</u> won <u>its</u> first game of the season.
> (reference to one team)

> Our <u>group</u> were asked <u>their</u> preferences.
> (reference to group as individuals)

3. Use a singular pronoun when two or more singular antecedents are joined by *or* or *nor*.

> Neither Ben <u>nor</u> Jim is in <u>his</u> office today.

4. Use a singular pronoun when referring to antecedents such as *anyone, everyone, each, every,* and *any.* In the past the masculine pronoun was recommended in these sentences. However, today the trend is to give balanced treatment to both sexes when the sentence is related to both and to change the sentence in some manner. For example, in a group of both men and women,

> instead of saying: "<u>Each</u> person will bring <u>his</u> recommendations tomorrow."

> change to either: "<u>Each</u> person will bring <u>his or her</u> recommendations tomorrow."

> *or*

> preferred method: "<u>All</u> persons will bring <u>their</u> recommendations tomorrow."

5. Be sure the pronoun clearly refers to its antecedent. Otherwise, the sentence will have to be revised.

> **Unclear:**   Jeff told Mr. Mason that his vacation will begin on March 8. (Cannot tell whether <u>his</u> refers to Jeff or to Mr. Mason)

> **Clear:**   According to Jeff, Mr. Mason's vacation will begin on March 8.

> *or*

> Mr. Mason was told that Jeff's vacation will begin on March 8.

RELATED ASSIGNMENT:	EXERCISE 2.5, PAGE 33
	EXERCISE 2.6, PAGE 34

■ PARALLEL CONSTRUCTION

Ideas of equal importance in a sentence should be worded in the same grammatical form; that is, the constructions should be parallel. For instance, a listing of activities you have planned could be worded as *infinitives* (the word *to* followed by a verb) or as *verbals* or *gerunds* (an *ing* word used as a noun); but one listing should not include more than one grammatical form. Sentences with parallel constructions are easy to read and understand. Sentences that are not parallel are often confusing to the reader.

Incorrect construction using infinitives:

> Our current goals should be <u>to</u> work hard, <u>to</u> produce a quality product, and maintain a good attitude.

Correct construction using infinitives:

> Our current goals should be <u>to</u> work hard, <u>to</u> produce a quality product, and <u>to</u> maintain a good attitude.

Incorrect construction using verbals or gerunds:

> Our current goals should include work<u>ing</u> hard, produc<u>ing</u> a quality product, and to maintain a good attitude.

Correct construction using verbals or gerunds:

> Our current goals should include work<u>ing</u> hard, produc<u>ing</u> a quality product, and maintain<u>ing</u> a good attitude.

■ SPLIT INFINITIVES

Split infinitives occur when at least one word is placed between the *to* and the verb. If possible, the infinitive should be kept together.

Split infinitive: Lorenz was asked <u>to not go</u> to the seminar.

Correct: Lorenz was asked <u>not to go</u> to the seminar.

■ VERBAL MODIFIERS

Verbal nouns (gerunds) may be modified by another noun or pronoun to show ownership. The modifying noun or pronoun used must be in possessive case.

Incorrect: We appreciate <u>you</u> making this correction.

Correct: We appreciate <u>your</u> making this correction.

■ DANGLING MODIFIERS

Dangling modifiers occur when a phrase used at the beginning of a sentence does not modify the subject of the sentence.

Dangling modifier: <u>Having completed the project</u>, an expense <u>report</u> was submitted by the director.

Correct: <u>Having completed the project</u>, the <u>director</u> submitted an expense report.

RELATED ASSIGNMENT: EXERCISE 2.7,   PAGE 35
                             EXERCISE 2.8,   PAGE 36

■ VOICE

Voice indicates whether the subject of the sentence is doing or receiving the action described by the verb. If the subject does the action, the sentence is in the *active* voice. If the subject receives the action, the sentence is in the *passive* voice. ■

> Mr. Wilson wrote this report.   (active voice)
>
> This report was written by Mr. Wilson.   (passive voice)

The active voice is more direct and emphatic than the passive voice and is also less wordy. Use of the active voice is preferred in most writing.

The passive voice is necessary in some instances. It is used if the receiver of the action is more important than the doer; if the doer is unknown or unnecessary; and for reasons of tact.

> The president of the company was elected by the members of the board.   (receiver more important than doer)
>
> The error was discovered the next day.   (doer unknown)
>
> Your payment has not been received.   (more tactful than ''You failed to send your payment.'')

Except in these instances, the passive voice should be avoided. It can greatly weaken the effectiveness of a message. The active voice and the passive voice should not be used in the same sentence.

Remember always to check with the author before making changes if you are unsure of the intended meaning of a message.

END-OF-CHAPTER ASSIGNMENT:	EXERCISE 2.9, PAGE 37
	EXERCISE 2.10, PAGE 38

▤ EXERCISE 2.1

Complete the exercise below to practice checking the grammatical construction of sentences. For each pair of sentences, determine which is a complete sentence. Place an X to the right of the correctly constructed sentence in each pair.

1. a. To determine the mathematical accuracy of the calculations. _____

    b. Please determine the mathematical accuracy of the calculations. _____

2. a. Because the land is in a good location and the price has recently been reduced. _____

    b. The land is in a good location, and the price has recently been reduced. _____

3. a. The building is located on Thompson Street and has a large oak tree in the center of the courtyard. _____

    b. The house that is located on Thompson Street and that has a large oak tree in the center of the courtyard. _____

4. a. Having completed their work, the secretaries attending the reception. _____

    b. Having completed their work, the secretaries attended the reception. _____

5. a. One representative, whose home office is in Atlanta, went to the national meeting. _____

    b. One representative, whose home office is in Atlanta, and went to the national meeting. _____

🮑 EXERCISE   2.2

Complete the exercise below to practice proofreading the grammatical construction of sentences. Read the paragraph and use revision marks to indicate errors. Then rewrite or retype the paragraph correctly in the space provided. Be sure to proofread your final copy.

Career paths for traditional executive assistants vary according to the size and attitude of the particular firm. In some cases, assistants beginning in typing pools or as assistants to junior executives. As their skills increase, these executive assistants given jobs working for middle or upper management. Or they may be promoted when their employers are promoted. Eventually, may work for only one person. They may be ask to do some supervisory work.

▤ EXERCISE   2.3

Complete the exercise below to review rules for agreement of subject and verb. Read each sentence and determine which word in parentheses is the appropriate verb. Circle the correct verb in each sentence.

1. All employees (is, are) expected to arrive at work on time.

2. Fred Smith and Abraham Plunkett (is, are) new members of the group.

3. The seminar leader (seem, seems) pleased with our participation.

4. Either Jake or his father (is, are) going to do the repair work.

5. As treasurer of the organization, you (is, are) required to prepare the financial statements.

6. The president, as well as the members of the board of directors, (has, have) decided to attend the meeting in Tokyo.

7. Each of the committee members (is, are) in favor of the amendment.

8. Marilyn (say, says) she is happy at her new job.

9. Neither Larry nor the other students (was, were) able to stay after school to work on the project.

10. The total of the contributions for this month's fund drive (is, are) $1,385.42.

11. Everyone who participated in the activities (has, have) a new understanding of the equipment.

12. Jerry usually (ask, asks) many questions during board meetings.

13. A new shipment of purchase order forms (is, are) expected to be received today.

14. Only one of the workers (want, wants) to work on Saturday.

15. All the current members (joins, join) me in welcoming you.

📋 EXERCISE   2.4

Complete the exercise below to practice proofreading for agreement of subject and verb. Read the paragraph and use revision marks to indicate errors. Then rewrite or retype the paragraph correctly in the space provided. Be sure to proofread your final copy.

Here is your instructions for handling money received in the mail. If an enclosure in a letter is money, be sure that the amount received match the amount mentioned in the letter. When it do not agree, write the amount received and the difference in the margin of the letter. All checks, money orders, and cash is turned over to the cashier twice daily. Keep an accurate record to show that the amount you receive balances with the amount you submits to the cashier.

▤ EXERCISE 2.5

Complete the exercise below to review rules for agreement of pronouns and their antecedents. Read each sentence and determine which word in parentheses is the appropriate pronoun. Circle the correct pronoun in each sentence.

1. Each person was asked to place (his or her, their) signature on the personnel form.

2. Each of the mechanics must provide (his or her, their) own repair tools.

3. The company volleyball team completed (its, their) season last week.

4. All the keyboard operators completed (his or her, their) assignments.

5. Neither Jane nor Mary participated in (her/their) department's meeting.

6. Both Frank and Rita have taken (his or her, their) vacations.

7. Neither the department heads nor the plant managers wanted (his or her, their) yearly budgets reduced.

8. Either Karen or the other members will report (his or her, their) findings at the next meeting.

9. The management staff has completed (its, their) budget reports for the current year.

10. The research and development group are signing (its, their) yearly travel request forms.

11. Mr. Hernandez, along with the other members of his staff, will receive (his, their) sales awards at the banquet.

12. Six typists, along with the word processing supervisor, will soon be moving to (his or her, their) new office.

13. All new employees, including George, will order (his, their) uniforms next Thursday.

14. Our firm has recently begun advertising for electrical engineers for (its, their) Seattle Plant.

15. As soon as the order for new books has been typed, please send (it, them) to the purchasing department.

▤ EXERCISE

Complete the exercise below to practice proofreading for agreement of pronouns and their antecedents. Read the paragraph and use revision marks to indicate errors. Then rewrite or retype the paragraph correctly in the space provided. Be sure to proofread your final copy.

Listening is a very important skill. Studies show that the average person spends a majority of their day in communicating. About half of that time, he or she is listening. Businesses consider listening to be an essential skill for their office workers. Studies also show that within two months after a person hears information, they remember only about one fourth of it.

📋 EXERCISE   2.7

Complete the exercise below to practice proofreading for parallel construction. Determine which sentences are correctly written and which need to be revised. If the sentence is correct, place a C in the column on the right. If the sentence should be revised, mark any changes; then rewrite or retype it in the space below the sentence. Be sure to proofread your final copy.

1. My favorite tasks are to type letters and filing invoices.   _____

2. The receptionist's jobs include answering the telephone and
    greeting visitors.   _____

3. Either work late tonight or you could work extra hours on
    Saturday.   _____

4. Most of our manuals are designed to help new employees
    learn our practices and give them a chance to work on their
    own.   _____

5. Angelo's goals for the week were to read three reports, to
    complete his budget, and he also planned to go to Dallas to a
    meeting.   _____

▤ EXERCISE   2.8

Complete the exercise below to practice proofreading for parallel construction, split infinitives, and dangling modifiers. Read the paragraph and use revision marks to indicate errors. Then rewrite or retype the paragraph correctly in the space provided. Be sure to proofread your final copy.

Listening is the process by which oral language is received, recognized, comprehended, and is retained. The main aspects of listening are not located in the ears. Our listening is based on our needs, desires, interests, and our previous experiences. While listening, our thoughts flow into ideas and emotions and therefore affecting what we hear. We have a tendency to not listen to subjects we dislike. Three elements of the listening process are attention, comprehending, and retention.

▤ EXERCISE 2.9

Complete the exercise below to check your ability to proofread material containing a variety of grammatical errors. Use revision marks to indicate errors. Rewrite or retype this material on another page. Be sure to proofread your final copy.

MEMORANDUM

TO: All Employees

FROM: Janice Washington, Personnel

DATE: January 15, 19--

SUBJECT: Vacation Schedules

Requests for vacation dates is now being accepted.   Each employee must complete the appropriate request form and have it approved by their immediate supervisor.   These request must be signed by both the supervisor and the employee, they must include a first choice and a second choice, and be sure to submit two copies.

Those employees whose requests are turned in within the next two weeks will be given first priority in his/her requests.

Thanking you for your cooperation.

gl

▤ EXERCISE   2.10

Complete the exercise below to check your ability to proofread material containing a variety of grammatical errors. Use revision marks to indicate errors. Rewrite or retype this material on another page. Be sure to proofread your final copy.

1222 Arrowhead
Sand Springs, OK 74022
March 15, 19--

Ms. Evelyn Mitchell
Jennings, Brown, Mitchell, and Long
1107 Boston
Tulsa, OK 74102

Dear Ms. Mitchell:

Your advertisement for a legal administrator trainee in the Sunday newspaper were of interest to me because I is about to complete my degree in law office management and are interested in working for a firm with a fine reputation such as yours.

While attending college, I also works temporarily at several local law firms to helps me gain experience in the legal world. Being involved in several activities while in school, helping me to develop skills of leadership, accepting responsibilities, and initiative.

I have specialized my studies somewhat in the area of litigation, which one of my instructors say is the field in which your firm specializes. I believe my education, work experience, and being interested in achieving would fit in well with your organization.

Please review the attached data sheet and contact me about a time we could meet to further discuss the possibility of my working for your firm as a legal administrator trainee.

Sincerely,

Terry Katz

grl

Enclosure

<h1>Chapter</h1>

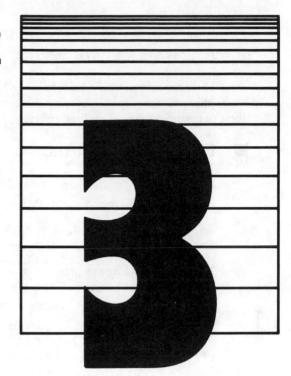

SPELLING

What's Wrong Here?

Stated in a sales letter to a teacher: The enclosed materials would provide a compliment to your current text.

■ NEED FOR STUDYING SPELLING

It is obvious that you have to know the correct spellings of words to know when they are presented correctly (or incorrectly) on a page. To be a good proofreader, you must be able to recognize spelling errors.

    Dictionaries and other word reference books are extremely helpful in checking spellings, but have you ever heard someone complain that a dictionary is of little use if you don't already know how to spell the word? You must have a good idea what letters are in a word before you can find it in the dictionary. Knowledge of some basic spelling rules can help you solve that problem.

    When in doubt, *always* check the spelling in a reference book. ■

    The correct spelling of names and addresses is equally important. You must spell names of persons and businesses accurately to maintain the credibility of your firm and to avoid offending the persons involved. Addresses must be correct to ensure prompt delivery. Be sure to check this information very carefully. Compare your document with other documents containing the information.

    Programs to check spelling are available for use with word processing equipment. The programs check the words you type against a list of correctly spelled words that are stored with the programs. Even with "spelling checker" programs, careful proofreading is necessary, because the programs have at least two major limitations:

1. They assume that any word used is misspelled if it does not match a word on the list.

2. They do not identify correctly spelled words that are used incorrectly.

There are several useful rules to help you with your spelling. Although there are the usual "exceptions to every rule," learning these rules can give you confidence and help you avoid some of the most common spelling errors.

■ FORMING PLURALS

1. The plural of most nouns is formed by adding *s*.

   typists   papers   mothers-in-law (add plural to main word)

2. In nouns ending in *s, z, ch, sh,* or *x*, add *es*.

   dresses   quizzes   churches   wishes   taxes

3. In nouns ending in *y* preceded by a consonant, change the *y* to *i* and add *es*. When the *y* is preceded by a vowel, keep the *y* and add *s*.

   marry to marries   county to counties   attorney to attorneys

4. Some nouns ending in *o* form the plural by adding *s* while others ending in *o* form the plural by adding *es*.
   A. In nouns ending in *o* preceded by a vowel, add *s* to form the plural.
      studios   patios   radios
   B. In nouns ending in *o* preceded by a consonant, the plural varies. Some add *s*, others add *es*.
      avocados   silos   tomatoes   potatoes

5. All musical terms ending in *o* form the plural by adding *s*.

   pianos   solos   concertos   altos

6. Some nouns ending in *f* or *fe* form the plural by adding *s* while others ending in *f* or *fe* form the plural by changing the *f* to *v* and adding *es*.

   reef to reefs   safe to safes   self to selves   elf to elves   knife to knives

There are exceptions to these guides; when in doubt about the plural form of a word, consult a dictionary.

RELATED ASSIGNMENT:	EXERCISE 3.1, PAGE 45

■ ADDING PREFIXES AND SUFFIXES

1. A prefix is added to the beginning of a word without changing the spelling of the root word. Listed below are examples of some frequently used prefixes.

prefix	meaning	example
bi	twice	bimonthly
co	together	coeducational
de	opposite	decentralize
dis	opposite	disobey
fore	before	forecast
mis	bad; wrong	misspell
non	not	nonfiction
post	after	postgraduate
pre	before	predawn
re	again	restate

2. A suffix is added to the end of a word, sometimes causing a change in the spelling of the root word. The last letter may be doubled, dropped, or changed to another letter. Listed below are examples of frequently used suffixes.

suffix	meaning	example
able	capable of being	knowledgeable
ary	having to do with	parliamentary
ation	act or process of	reformation
ed	in the past	walked
ee	person who is something	absentee
est	most	lightest
ing	act of	painting
like	characteristic of	businesslike
ment	act of	achievement
ship	office; condition	judgeship

3. When the root word is one syllable (or when the accent is on the last syllable) and the word ends with a single consonant preceded by a single vowel, double the final consonant before adding a suffix that begins with a vowel. Vowels are *a, e, i, o, u,* and *y* when *y* is pronounced like a long *i.*

    plan to planned   admit to admitted

    Note: This guide does not apply if the final consonant is silent.
              mow to mowing

    Reminder: According to the list of typical proofreading errors shown in Chapter 1, it is difficult to spot the omission of one doubled letter. When the letter has been added to create a suffix, it may be even more difficult to locate.

4. Drop the final *e* before adding a suffix beginning with a vowel.
    bake + ing = baking   move + able = movable

    Exceptions: The *e* is usually not dropped in words ending with the "soft" *c* or *g,* such as changeable and noticeable. In addition, the final *e* is sometimes omitted when adding a suffix beginning with a *consonant,* as in truly (true + ly).

    Note: The final *e* is kept when dropping it would cause confusion with another word.
              dye + ing = dyeing (not dying)

5. When the root word ends in *y* preceded by a consonant, change the *y* to *i* before adding a suffix—unless the suffix begins with i.

    carry changes to carrier or to carrying (not carriing)

6. When the root word ends in *ie,* change the *ie* to *y* before adding *ing.*
    lie + ing = lying

7. Only one word ends with *sede:*
    supersede

    Only three words end with *ceed:*
    exceed, proceed, succeed

    All other words with this "seed" sound in the ending are spelled *cede.*
    precede   recede   accede

RELATED ASSIGNMENT: **EXERCISE 3.2,   PAGE 46**

■ CHOOSING *IE* OR *EI*

Remember the poem—

I before E except after C, or when sounded like A as in neighbor and weigh.

This poem refers to words in which the *ie* or *ei* combination has only one sound—usually the long *e*.

Examples of *ie* words (long *e* sound):

> field   achieve   believe

Examples of *ei* words (long *a* sound or after a *c*):

> freight   deceive   receive

Keep in mind that there are exceptions to the *ie/ei* poem. Watch for them; learn to spell them or keep a reference book handy. Learning to spell them is much faster than looking them up!

Examples of exceptions:

> foreign   either   leisure   caffeine

Reminder: It is difficult to locate transposed letters; when the error involves letters such as *i* and *e* that are often used in both combinations, the error is especially difficult to notice.

RELATED ASSIGNMENT:	**EXERCISE 3.3, PAGE 47**

■ FOLLOWING PRONUNCIATION GUIDES

Pronouncing a word correctly usually helps you to spell it correctly. Listed below are some words that are frequently misspelled simply because they are mispronounced. Practice pronouncing them correctly to ensure spelling them correctly.

ask	(not ax)
athletic	(3 syllables; not ath-e-let-ic)
chimney	(2 syllables; not chim-e-ney)
congratulations	(t in middle; no d)
disastrous	(3 syllables; not dis-as-ter-ous)
drowned	(1 syllable; not drownded)
hundred	(not hunderd)
incidentally	(5 syllables; not incidently)
mischievous	(only 3 syllables)
nuclear	(not nucular)
once	(no t sound at end of word)
perform	(not preform)
realty	(not re-li-ty)
recognize	(cog in middle)
relevant	(not revalent)

■ USING SPELLING LISTS

Review the list of frequently misspelled words on page 43. Studying lists of this type can help you learn to spell the words correctly. Your goal is to train your eyes so that only the correct form of each word looks proper. Writing three times those words that give you difficulty will help you learn to spell them correctly.

END-OF-CHAPTER ASSIGNMENT:	**EXERCISES 3.4 THROUGH 3.10, PAGES 48 THROUGH 54.**

■ FREQUENTLY MISSPELLED WORDS

1. absence
2. accessible
3. accommodate
4. accompanying
5. accumulate
6. achievement
7. acknowledge
8. acknowledgment
9. across
10. advisable
11. all right
12. altogether
13. apparent
14. appraisal
15. argument
16. article
17. attachment
18. attorneys
19. auditor
20. auxiliary
21. bankruptcy
22. bargain
23. beginning
24. believe
25. beneficial
26. beneficiary
27. benefited
28. biennium
29. bookkeeper
30. brochure
31. budgetary
32. bulletin
33. bureaucrat
34. cancellation
35. capitalize
36. category
37. chargeable
38. charitable
39. clientele
40. comparative
41. comprehensive
42. concede
43. congratulate
44. conscientious
45. conscious
46. consecutive
47. consensus
48. consistent
49. contingency
50. controversial
51. convenience
52. convertible
53. correspondence
54. courteous
55. credibility
56. criticism
57. defendant
58. deficiency
59. definite
60. dependent
61. desirable
62. development
63. dilemma
64. disappoint
65. discrepancy
66. efficient
67. elementary
68. eligible
69. embarrass
70. endeavor
71. environment
72. equipped
73. especially
74. exceed
75. excellent
76. exhaust
77. exorbitant
78. experience
79. extortion
80. extraordinary
81. facsimile
82. familiar
83. fascinated
84. feasibility
85. feasible
86. February
87. financial
88. fiscal
89. flexible
90. fluorescent
91. forecast
92. foreclosure
93. foreign
94. foreseeable
95. foresight
96. forfeit
97. fulfill
98. genuine
99. government
100. governor
101. gracious
102. grateful
103. grievance
104. guarantee
105. harass
106. hazardous
107. illegible
108. impartial
109. implement
110. incidentally
111. indebtedness
112. indispensable
113. infallible
114. intangible
115. interfered
116. itinerary
117. jeopardize
118. journeys
119. knowledgeable
120. legible
121. leisure
122. liaison
123. license
124. maintenance
125. manufacture
126. miscellaneous
127. mortgage
128. necessary
129. noticeable
130. nuisance
131. obsolete
132. obstacle
133. occasion
134. occurrence
135. pamphlet
136. parallel
137. parliamentary
138. permanent
139. perseverance
140. personnel
141. pneumatic
142. precede
143. precedent
144. prerequisite
145. prerogative
146. prevalent
147. privilege
148. procedure
149. proceed
150. promissory
151. propaganda
152. quantity
153. questionnaire
154. receive
155. recipient
156. recommend
157. referred
158. rehabilitation
159. relevant
160. requisition
161. rescind
162. restaurant
163. schedule
164. separate
165. similar
166. simultaneous
167. sincerely
168. skillful
169. subpoena
170. supersede
171. tariff
172. temperature
173. tragedy
174. transferring
175. truly
176. unmanageable
177. unprecedented
178. vacuum
179. versatile
180. yield

▤ EXERCISE   3.1

In the blank spaces provided, write the correct spelling of the plural form of each word.

1. curio   _____

2. approach   _____

3. baby   _____

4. cost   _____

5. dish   _____

6. inquiry   _____

7. shelf   _____

8. brother-in-law   _____

9. soprano   _____

10. attorney   _____

▤ EXERCISE 3.2

In the blank spaces provided, write the correct spelling of each word by adding prefixes and suffixes as indicated.

1. value + able _____

2. singe + ing _____

3. un + necessary _____

4. sad + est _____

5. hope + ing _____

6. care + ful _____

7. mis + spell _____

8. die + ing _____

9. row + ing _____

10. commit + ed _____

▤ EXERCISE

Study each word listed below. If the word is spelled correctly, write C in the answer column. If it is incorrectly spelled, write the correct spelling in the answer column.

1. conscience _____

2. recieve _____

3. weird _____

4. mischievous _____

5. thier _____

6. sheik _____

7. forfiet _____

8. seize _____

9. shreik _____

10. vein _____

NAME

EXERCISE 3.4

Read the words in each pair and determine which is the correct spelling. Circle the correctly spelled word in each pair.

1. a. accessable
   b. accessible

2. a. accummulate
   b. accumulate

3. a. all right
   b. alright

4. a. arguement
   b. argument

5. a. auxiliary
   b. auxillary

6. a. bookeeper
   b. bookkeeper

7. a. catagory
   b. category

8. a. congradulate
   b. congratulate

9. a. concensus
   b. consensus

10. a. defendant
    b. defendent

11. a. desirable
    b. desireable

12. a. disappoint
    b. dissapoint

13. a. especially
    b. expecially

14. a. exhorbitant
    b. exorbitant

15. a. feasability
    b. feasibility

16. a. February
    b. Febuary

17. a. forefeit
    b. forfeit

18. a. interfered
    b. interferred

19. a. liaison
    b. liason

20. a. neccessary
    b. necessary

21. a. ocassion
    b. occasion

22. a. paralell
    b. parallel

23. a. personell
    b. personnel

24. a. precede
    b. preceed

25. a. priviledge
    b. privilege

26. a. questionaire
    b. questionnaire

27. a. similar
    b. similiar

▤ EXERCISE   3.5

Read the words in each group and determine which are spelled correctly. Write a C beside the correctly spelled words, and write the correct spelling beside any incorrectly spelled word. It is possible that no words in a group are misspelled or that all are misspelled.

1. a. advisable _____
   b. apparent _____
   c. alltogether _____
   d. achievement _____

2. a. accummulate _____
   b. attorneys _____
   c. argument _____
   d. auxillary _____

3. a. bargain _____
   b. bureaucrat _____
   c. bookeeper _____
   d. bankrupcy _____

4. a. category _____
   b. concientous _____
   c. convienience _____
   d. conceed _____

5. a. development _____
   b. dependant _____
   c. desireable _____
   d. disappoint _____

6. a. embarass _____
   b. endeavor _____
   c. enviornment _____
   d. expecially _____

7. a. fullfill _____
   b. feasable _____
   c. forclosure _____
   d. florescent _____

8. a. guarantee _____
   b. gracious _____
   c. goverment _____
   d. greatful _____

9. a. illedgible _____
   b. implement _____
   c. indispensible _____
   d. itinerary _____

10. a. license _____
    b. leisure _____
    c. liason _____
    d. legible _____

▤ EXERCISE   3.6

Read the words in each group and determine which are spelled correctly. Write a C beside the correctly spelled words, and write the correct spelling beside any incorrectly spelled word. It is possible that no words in a group are misspelled or that all are misspelled.

1. a. maintenence _____
    b. manufacture _____
    c. miscelaneous _____
    d. mortgage _____

2. a. obsolete _____
    b. occurrence _____
    c. obstacle _____
    d. occasion _____

3. a. permanent _____
    b. paralell _____
    c. personnell _____
    d. procede _____

4. a. propaganda _____
    b. priviledge _____
    c. prerogative _____
    d. promissary _____

5. a. relavant _____
    b. recipient _____
    c. reccommend _____
    d. receive _____

6. a. rehabilitation _____
    b. restaurent _____
    c. rescind _____
    d. recquisition _____

7. a. skillful _____
    b. similiar _____
    c. seperate _____
    d. schedule _____

8. a. supercede _____
    b. subpoena _____
    c. simulatneous _____
    d. supoena _____

9. a. tragedy _____
    b. truely _____
    c. temperature _____
    d. tarriff _____

10. a. unmanagable _____
    b. vacuum _____
    c. unprecedented _____
    d. versatill _____

▤ EXERCISE   3.7

Read the paragraph and use revision marks to indicate any misspelled words. Rewrite or retype the paragraph correctly in the remaining space. Be sure to proofread your final copy.

Thank you for your courteous letter asking for information about our restaurant. We would be greatful if you would find it feasable to visit us in the foreseeable future. We can guarantee to provide excellent, efficient service and extroardinary food in a pleasant enviornment. The attatchment is a broshure showing our gracious dining room with a listing of our scheduled hours of operation.

🖹 EXERCISE 3.8

Read the paragraph and use revision marks to indicate any misspelled words. Rewrite or retype the paragraph correctly in the remaining space. Be sure to proofread your final copy.

Three months have passed and we have not recieved your chek for $50 for the meal you ate with us. Perhaps there is a discrepency between your bookeeper's records and ours. This indebtedness may jeopardize your credit, and we think it is adviseable for you to clear up this apparant oversight so we will not have to institute legal procedures through our attornies. Incidentally, thank you for fulfilling our request for the questionnaire.

▤ EXERCISE

Complete the exercise below to practice proofreading for errors in spelling. Read the memo and use revision marks to indicate errors. Rewrite or retype this information on another page. Be sure to proofread your final copy.

```
MEMORANDUM

TO:        Marsorie Maddox

FROM:      Josephine Davis

SUBJECT:   Recent Accomplishments

DATE:      July 7, 19--


Consradulations on your recent recosnition as recipient of
the city's humanitarian award. We have all benefitted from
your excellent work and are expecially pleased at this
achievement.

Your excellent and conscientous work durins the recent train
tradsedy should suarantee you a recommendation from the
sovernor for a similiar award from the state.

We are srateful for your efficient and Knowledsable handlins
of this unusual occurrence.

srl
```

▤ EXERCISE   3.10

Complete the exercise below to practice proofreading for errors in spelling. Read the letter and use revision marks to indicate errors. Rewrite or retype this letter on another page. Be sure to proofread your final copy.

1707 Beechwood
Tyler, TX 75702
January 25, 19--

Mr. William Cantrell
P. O. Box 1121
College Station, TX 77841

Dear Mr. Cantrell:

Thank you for your recent letter regarding our personnel needs. It would be a priviledge to talk with you at your convenience.

We would appreciate your completing the attached questionnaire so we can procede with the necessary paperwork. Once this material is recieved, we will make definite plans for a meeting.

Please let us know your Febuary itinerary.

Sincerly,

John J. Duke
Personnel Manager

js

Attachment

Chapter

PUNCTUATION

 ## What's Wrong Here?

Typed in a progress report: **The menu for the banquet includes a half-baked chicken.**

■ IMPORTANCE OF PUNCTUATION

Punctuation marks help make sentences clear. Incorrectly placed or omitted punctuation marks make the message difficult to understand. They can even change the intended meaning.

Guides for the use of various punctuation marks are described in the remainder of this chapter. For additional rules and examples, consult a standard reference manual.

■ PERIODS (.)

1. Use a period to mark the end of most sentences, including statements of fact, commands, and polite requests.

> Your performance evaluation report has been completed.
> (statement of fact)
>
> Send your response to Mae Francis.
> (command)
>
> Would you please confirm your arrival time.
> (polite request)

2. Use a period after initials and after some abbreviations. Since the use of periods with abbreviations varies so much, consult a reference manual when in doubt or follow the organization's practice.

> Joe F. Ballentino (period after initial)
> Jerry Allen, Ph.D. (period after abbreviation)
> etc. (period after abbreviation)
> Sallisaw, OK (no period after two-letter state abbreviation)

RELATED ASSIGNMENT:	EXERCISE 4.1,	PAGE 61

■ QUESTION MARKS (?) AND EXCLAMATION POINTS (!)

1. Use a question mark after a direct question.

> When will you return from the conference?

2. Use an exclamation point to show emotion or strong feeling. This punctuation mark can be used after words, phrases, or complete sentences. Exclamation points are not widely used in standard business correspondence. Using too many exclamation points weakens their impact and is distracting to the reader.

> Hurry! The meeting has already started!

RELATED ASSIGNMENT:	EXERCISE 4.2,	PAGE 62

■ COMMAS (,)

1. Use a comma to separate two independent clauses that are joined by a conjunction (*and, but, or, nor, for*) if there are no other commas within the clauses. (An *independent clause* contains a subject and a verb and can stand alone as a complete sentence.) When commas are used within either clause, a semicolon is used to separate them.

> Letitia is a very enthusiastic employee, and her work has improved.
>
> (two independent clauses)
>
> Francesca has been hired as office manager and will supervise seven workers.
>
> (one independent clause)

2. Use a comma to separate items in a series. These items may be individual words, phrases, clauses, or numbers.

> Speakers at the meeting will be Larry Henderson, Jackie Long, and Karen Katz.
>
> Prices for the new inventory items will be $1.25, $7.60, and $10.97.

3. Use a comma to separate introductory words, phrases, and dependent clauses from the main part of the sentence. (A *dependent clause* cannot stand alone as a sentence.)

> Surprisingly, production is expected to increase next year.
>
> As you may know, three new branches will open in October.

4. Use a comma to set off parenthetical expressions. (Parenthetical expressions are words or phrases that can be removed without changing the meaning of a sentence.)

> The new office supplies, however, will not be delivered this week.

> Expansion of our computer facilities, of course, will be included in next year's budget.

5. Use a comma to separate parts of a date when the date includes month, day, and year. Also include a comma after the year when the year is not at the end of the sentence. If the day is given before the month, no comma is needed between the day and the month.

> July 4, 1776, was a memorable day.

> The documents were delivered on the 16th of May, 1984.

6. Use commas to set off appositives from the rest of the sentence. (*Appositive:* Explanatory information that can be omitted without changing the meaning of the sentence.)

> Dianne Stratton, a systems consultant, will visit our office today.

> The chairman of the fund drive, Gary Giovanni, will give a progress report at tomorrow's meeting.

7. Use a comma to separate two equal, consecutive adjectives modifying one noun. If the word *and* can be inserted between the two adjectives, the words are considered equal.

> The word processing office contains modern, efficient equipment.

> A review of our plant facilities showed that we are providing a safe, secure working environment.

8. Use a comma to separate two independent, consecutive numbers; the preferred alternative is to rearrange the sentence.

> On October 10, 25 students will tour our offices.

> Twenty-five students will tour our offices on October 10.

| RELATED ASSIGNMENT: | EXERCISE 4.3, PAGE 63 |
| | EXERCISE 4.4, PAGE 64 |

■ SEMICOLONS (;) AND COLONS (:)

1. Use a semicolon between two independent clauses in a sentence when no conjunction is used. (Reminder: Conjunctions are *and, but, or, for, nor.*)

> Our Toronto office had the highest sales last year; Boston was second in sales.

> Our office will be closed two days this month for holidays; however, employees will be paid for the entire month.

2. Use a semicolon before the conjunction to separate two independent clauses if either clause already contains a comma.

> After net earnings are determined, I will finish the annual report; and James will prepare the financial statements.

3. Use a semicolon in place of a comma to separate items in a series if any of the items already contain a comma.

> Our visiting directors will be coming from Des Moines, Iowa; Savannah, Georgia; and Birmingham, Alabama.

4. Use a semicolon, commas, and rewording as needed to correct run-on sentences. A run-on sentence usually occurs when too many words or ideas have been placed in one sentence.

Run-on sentence: He purchased a new calculator and he had it shipped to the main office because their old machine was too slow and it needed to be repaired.

Correction: He purchased a new calculator and had it shipped to the main office; their old machine was too slow, and it needed to be repaired.

5. Use a colon to introduce a list or series, an example, or a long quotation.

> Please send the following information: the number of copies desired, the size of print preferred, and the color of paper to be used.

Exceptions:

A. When the introductory information before a listing is a transitional expression rather than an independent clause, use a semicolon before and a comma after the introductory expression.

> Several reproduction methods are available; for example,
> 1. photocopies
> 2. stencil duplicator
> 3. offset printer

B. When another sentence separates the introductory sentence from the listing, use a period at the end of the introduction.

> The following representatives will attend.
> They will arrive Tuesday, May 5.
> 1. Pete Andeopolous
> 2. Meredith McHenry
> 3. Luiz Lorenzo

C. When a listing is introduced with a *being* verb, such as *is, are,* or *were,* use no punctuation.

> Our preferred meeting dates are
> 1. May 17
> 2. July 10
> 3. August 11

RELATED ASSIGNMENT:	EXERCISE 4.5,	PAGE 65

■ APOSTROPHE (') AND QUOTATION MARKS (")

1. Use an apostrophe to show possession. Add an apostrophe and an s to make a singular noun possessive and to make possessive those plural nouns not ending in an s or z sound. Add an apostrophe to make possessive those plural nouns ending in an s or z sound.

> One employee's personnel folder was misplaced. (singular)
> The men's basketball team will practice Friday evening. (plural)
> The employees' lounge will be remodeled in January. (plural)

2. Use quotation marks to enclose short, direct quotations. Also use quotation marks for parts of books or parts of magazines. Note these special punctuation rules:

A. Commas and periods are always placed *inside* quotation marks.
   President Reid stated, ''All clerical employees are to report to work half an hour early on Friday.''

B. Colons and semicolons are always placed *outside* quotation marks.
   The book contains an interesting section on ''Electronic Mail Equipment''; please read it by Monday.

C. Exclamation points and question marks go *inside* when they belong with the quoted words only and *outside* when they belong with the entire sentence.
   Mr. Smith asked, ''What time is the meeting?''
   Did you report on the article, ''Artificial Intelligence''?

RELATED ASSIGNMENT:	**EXERCISE 4.6, PAGE 66**

■ HYPHENS (-) AND DASHES (--)

1. Use hyphens for adjectives joined as one unit to modify a noun.

   Please order the most up-to-date machinery.

2. Use hyphens for words with the prefixes *ex* and *self*.

   The ex-president will be present for the presentation.

   Our receptionists must be self-confident.

3. Use hyphens for numbers above 20 and below 100 when they are spelled out.

   Thirty-two of our employees prefer additional health coverage.

4. Use hyphens for fractions used as *adjectives, adverbs,* or *nouns*.

   One-half of the employees attended the picnic.

   A two-thirds vote is required for passage.

5. Use hyphens to divide a word at the end of a line.

   Friday is the dead-
   line for submitting
   expense reports.

6. Use dashes for emphasis or to set off parenthetical expressions that already contain commas. Dashes are typed as two hyphens. No space is left before or after the dash.

   Our committee meeting will be held Wednesday--not Thursday.

   Three of our sales offices--Atlanta, Houston, and Memphis--reached new sales records last month.

Additional guidelines for word division are presented in Chapter 11.

■ PARENTHESES

1. Parentheses are used to set off explanatory information from the rest of a sentence. The punctuation marks described in the early paragraphs of this chapter are illustrated by placing them within parentheses.

Comma (,)

2. Parentheses should be used only when necessary for explanatory information. Because they de-emphasize the information within them, parentheses can slow the reading rate and make the main message more difficult to follow. Other punctuation marks are preferred in most cases.

Parentheses preferred: The dollar sign ($) should be included when typing totals.

Other punctuation preferred: The new clerks were from three states: Idaho, Wyoming, and Colorado.

instead of

The new clerks were from three states (Idaho, Wyoming, and Colorado).

RELATED ASSIGNMENT:	EXERCISE 4.7, PAGE 67

END-OF-CHAPTER ASSIGNMENT:	EXERCISE 4.8 THROUGH 4.10, PAGES 68 THROUGH 70.

▤ EXERCISE

Complete the exercise below to practice proofreading sentence punctuation. Use revision marks to indicate any needed corrections. Some sentences may be correctly punctuated.

1. Jerry F Smith will be visiting our Newark office on December 5.

2. Please send us your check this week.

3. I would appreciate hearing from you on this matter

4. Would you please turn in your report by Friday?

5. Gary Flynn is moving to Ft. Worth.

6. The applicant for the managerial opening is Roberta Simmons, PhD.

7. The receptionist is Terry A. Mason.

8. May I please have the sample materials by April 2.

9. Lynn Barton received a perfect attendance award

10. The new staff physician is Dr Jackson P Lucas.

▤ EXERCISE 4.2

Complete the exercise below to practice proofreading sentence punctuation. Use revision marks to indicate any needed corrections. Some sentences may be correctly punctuated.

1. Will you be in your office later today.

2. Please send me your suggestions for improvements?

3. When will the minutes of the last meeting be ready?

4. Please come to work early tomorrow?

5. Will John Wilson be returning this week?

6. Congratulations. You have been named employee of the month.

7. Have the documents from New York been received?

8. Thank you. Your presence at the meeting was very helpful.

9. Good news! We will be getting additional insurance coverage next year.

10. Will you please check the files for the latest estimate?

📄 EXERCISE

Complete the exercise below to practice proofreading sentence punctuation. Use revision marks to indicate any needed corrections. Some sentences may be correctly punctuated.

1. The number of copies needed is five, and the materials must be received Tuesday.

2. Psychologists can determine what traits and skills are needed to perform a job well, and can screen employees accordingly.

3. Our new employees include a file clerk, a receptionist, and a typist.

4. Unfortunately our new equipment will not be arriving until June.

5. The working hours of our night employees therefore will be changed.

6. Our last evaluation report was completed on March 11, 1985 and needs to be updated.

7. Benjamin Sumner, secretary-treasurer of the corporation will be speaking at noon today.

8. Our new manager of data processing, Lauren Maynard, will begin work today.

9. Our word processing employees are efficient, highly motivated workers.

10. We have received several interesting, business reports this week.

▤ EXERCISE

Complete the exercise below to practice proofreading punctuation. Use revision marks to indicate any needed corrections. Rewrite or retype the paragraph in the space at the bottom of the page. Be sure to proofread your final copy.

Abraham Maslow, a psychologist is associated with research related to employee motivation. The most basic human needs, according to Maslow include food, drink, and shelter. These basic needs do not motivate employees after such needs have been satisfied. Another type of need then becomes a motivator and this need is usually for friendship and association with others. This type of need eventually loses its motivating power but another type of need becomes a motivator. A good supervisor of course must be aware of the appropriate motivators for each employee.

🔳 EXERCISE   4.5

Complete the exercise below to practice proofreading sentence punctuation. Use revision marks to indicate any needed corrections. Some sentences may be correctly punctuated.

1. Our sales have increased this month, however, our expenses have also increased.

2. The financial reports will be published Friday, and stockholders should be pleased.

3. Your report should include the following, a title page, a summary of results, and a recommendation.

4. Morgan will present the sales proposal; and Leonard will present the manufacturing report.

5. Unless the project is finished by Wednesday, we will have to ask for an extension of the deadline; and the contract will need to be revised.

6. New equipment was ordered from these firms: Royal, IBM, and Xerox.

7. After the end of the month, we will be able to install new lighting and new air conditioning.

8. New offices will be opening soon in Lincoln, Nebraska, Elgin, Illinois, and Detroit, Michigan.

9. The dates of the word processing seminars are as follows; May 3, June 15, and August 1.

10. Our main office; however, will remain in New York.

▤ EXERCISE

Complete the exercise below to practice proofreading sentence punctuation. Use revision marks to indicate any needed corrections. Some sentences may be correctly punctuated.

1. The receptionist's typewriter was replaced today.

2. One employees' paycheck was incorrect.

3. Our company presidents' secretary is on vacation this week.

4. All members' budget requests must be turned in by the end of the month.

5. A new mens' bowling league will be formed soon.

6. Please read this magazine article, "The Advantages of Electronic Mail.

7. A voice-activated typewriter, called a "VAT", is being developed for office use.

8. The head of the engineering division said, "All specifications for the project must be completed by noon tomorrow."

9. Do you know the meaning of the word "encryption?"

10. After checking the time, the supervisor said, "Hurry"!

🗏 EXERCISE 4.7

Complete the exercise below to practice proofreading sentence punctuation. Use revision marks to indicate any needed corrections. Some sentences may be correctly punctuated.

1. The assistant to the president is an ex-officio member of our committee.

2. One-fourth of the time was spent preparing the meeting agenda.

3. Fifty seven percent of our employees participated in our preventive health care plan.

4. Our records will soon be up-to-date.

5. Jeremy has promised to assist you with any last-minute details.

6. Roland Jablonski is the ex chairman of the board.

7. The renovation of the data processing section is two-thirds complete.

8. One-hundred employees are working at our Miami plant.

9. A percent sign, %, is not necessary in this table's total column.

10. Our goal is to make each plant self sufficient.

▤ EXERCISE

Complete the exercise below to practice proofreading punctuation. Use revision marks to indicate any needed corrections. Rewrite or retype the paragraph in the space at the bottom of the page. Be sure to proofread your final copy.

A new office worker is usually assigned the easiest tasks in the office. For example such trainees will be expected to learn what tasks are to be performed and who is to perform them. Each new employee should also learn the companys' policies; standards; and procedures. In the word processing center these are the three job levels; entry level worker, intermediate level worker, and experienced level worker. The supervisor may ask a new worker, "Will you be able to operate our telephone equipment"?

▤ EXERCISE 4.9

Complete the exercise below to check your ability to proofread material containing a variety of punctuation errors. Use revision marks to indicate errors. Rewrite or retype this information on another page. Be sure to proofread your final copy.

MEMORANDUM

TO: Word Processing Employees

FROM: Erlander James, Supervisor

DATE: May 12, 19--

SUBJECT: Employees' Duties

Some duties have changed for workers in the word processing center. Employees on Level 1 are expected to answer the telephone and take messages but they are not to place calls.   Telephone calls requesting information will be made by workers at Level 2 or Level 3 depending upon the difficulty of the problem.

Level 1 workers are also to maintain the office telephone directory, however these employees should not be responsible for confidential records.

Would you please be sure that new employees are given adequate training to handle entry-level assignments?

cb

▤ EXERCISE   4.10

Complete the exercise below to check your ability to proofread material containing a variety of
punctuation errors. Use revision marks to indicate errors. Rewrite or retype this letter on another
page. Be sure to proofread your final copy.

August 27, 19--

Mr. Wade K Gilbreth
4722 Hawthorne
Sacramento, CA. 95813

Dear Mr Gilbreth

Thank you for your letter asking for information about our latest product.

We are pleased that you have seen our commercials on television and we
hope you will continue buying our products.   As you have requested we are
sending you the following: an order form to be sent to our plant in Seattle,
Washington, a rebate coupon to be sent to our office in Reno, Nevada, and a
sample of our new product made in our plant in Topeka, Kansas.

According to our sales manager, "This is our best product ever"!

Sincerely

Lisbeth Marinello
Product Development

jc

Enclosure

Chapter

CAPITALIZATION

❓ What's Wrong Here?

Typed in a report: We visited the mobile plant yesterday.

Capitalization is used to identify sentence beginnings and proper nouns. Capitalization is also used for special emphasis. However, use of the underscore is usually more effective than capitalization for emphasizing entire words, phrases, or sentences.

Some variation exists in the use of capitalization. The trend today is toward decreased use of unnecessary capitalization, giving more emphasis to the items that *are* capitalized and making typing easier. ■

Listed below are the most widely accepted rules for capitalization.

1. Capitalize the first word of a sentence or a quotation.

   The automatic lights come on at sunset.
   The director said, ''All employees who donate to a local charity will receive a certificate from the company.''

2. Capitalize proper nouns, such as the names of people, places, and things.

   The president of Cabot International is Louis Lawhon.

3. Capitalize days of the week, months, and holidays.

   Our office will be closed Monday, September 3, for Labor Day.

RELATED ASSIGNMENT:	EXERCISE 5.1, PAGE 73
	EXERCISE 5.2, PAGE 74

4. Capitalize names of specific continents, countries, cities, states, and bodies of water. When more than one body of water is named, only the actual names are capitalized; words such as "river" and "ocean" are not capitalized.

> We called several cities in South America while we were at our plant in Houston, Texas.
> Our services are widely used in areas between the Atlantic Ocean and the Pacific Ocean.
> The Ohio and Mississippi rivers are widely used for barge transportation.

5. Capitalize historical documents and events.

> The Industrial Revolution caused many changes in the types of jobs available.

6. Capitalize a personal title when it immediately precedes a name in a sentence.

> The presentation will be made by Professor Ed Gilliam.
> The financial report will be given by Loren Graves, treasurer of the organization.

```
RELATED ASSIGNMENT:        EXERCISE 5.3,   PAGE 75
                           EXERCISE 5.4,   PAGE 76
```

7. Capitalize a title when used in an address or closing lines of a letter; capitalize the first word in a complimentary close.

> Mr. Abraham Bond, Coordinator
> Joint Products Division
> Davis Manufacturing
> New York, NY 10017
>
> Sincerely yours,
>
> Jacquelyn O'Riley, Group Leader

8. Capitalize compass points when they designate specific locations but not when they are used to show direction.

> The good weather in the South has helped speed the construction of our new plant. (indicates a location)
> Ponca City is 40 miles north of Stillwater. (indicates a direction)

9. A prefix or suffix added to a proper noun is not capitalized.

> The meeting was requested by ex-President Schiffelbein.
> President-elect Jemison will attend our next board meeting.

```
RELATED ASSIGNMENT:        EXERCISE 5.5,   PAGE 77
```

10. Follow your organization's practice in deciding other terms to capitalize, such as titles of officers and names of departments.

```
END-OF-CHAPTER            EXERCISES 5.6 THROUGH 5.10,
ASSIGNMENT:               PAGES 78 THROUGH 82.
```

📋 EXERCISE 5.1

Complete the exercise below to practice proofreading capitalization. Use revision marks to indicate any needed corrections. Some sentences may be correct.

1. New Year's day is a holiday at our firm.

2. The service representative said, "three of the machines cannot be repaired until new parts arrive."

3. Vicki Petre can be reached at her office every tuesday and wednesday.

4. Glenda p. Jerome is a new employee who will start work on monday, april 10.

5. Please send a copy of the report to Ed Merrill at Global industries.

6. Three of our employees are taking refresher courses at Cliffton community college.

7. Kenneth Framer will be attending the meeting as the representative from Hutton Hampton, inc.

8. Our offices will be open until noon on the day before thanksgiving.

9. Absenteeism is highest on mondays and fridays.

10. Our company's family outing will be held friday at Lincoln Park.

▤ EXERCISE   5.2

Complete the exercise below to practice proofreading capitalization. Use revision marks to indicate any needed corrections. Rewrite or retype the paragraph in the space provided at the bottom of the page. Be sure to proofread your final copy.

Our centralized copying service will now be open all day every monday through friday and until Noon each Saturday, excluding Holidays. Our new manager of this service is Sidney Schofield, who will be arriving Wednesday, August 10. He has previously worked in two of our other offices. Prior to joining our firm, sidney worked in a similar capacity for Logan electronics.

▤ EXERCISE

Complete the exercise below to practice proofreading capitalization. Use revision marks to indicate any needed corrections. Some sentences may be correct.

1. One location being considered for our international meeting is in south Africa.

2. Flooding has occurred near our plant in Arkansas because of the Mississippi river.

3. The presentation will be given by Nadine Morse, Secretary of the committee.

4. Our plants with the highest production last month were in Austin and Amarillo.

5. The Equal pay act has had an impact on the salaries in our offices.

6. The seminar about legislative changes will be presented by Representative Joyce Gallagher.

7. Safety awards were presented to employees at our plant in Joplin, Missouri.

8. Please check the time before calling our office in Foxboro, Massachusetts.

9. Plants similar to ours are being built in france and germany.

10. The meeting of the committee will be held in Toronto and will be directed by president Martha Lopez.

▤ EXERCISE 5.4

Complete the exercise below to practice proofreading capitalization. Use revision marks to indicate any needed corrections. Rewrite or retype the paragraph in the space at the bottom of the page. Be sure to proofread your final copy.

Plans are under way to modernize our data processing facilities in our New York and London offices. We will make a trip across the Ocean to England after the changes have been made there. Our safety codes will be reviewed and the plants inspected by Floyd Henderson, Director of the project. Final approval of the plans was given by president Tom Chapman last week in Los angeles.

☰ EXERCISE 5.5

Complete the exercise below to practice proofreading capitalization. Use revision marks to indicate any needed corrections. Some sentences may be correct.

1. Please use "Sincerely Yours" as the complimentary close for all my letters.

2. Many workers are available in the southwest to work in our new plant.

3. Our next meeting will be held in east Rutherford.

4. Repair work is being done to the West side of the office building.

5. Some employees have asked for transfers to locations in the western part of the state.

6. Please use "Samuel Blockhous, Administrative Assistant" as the writer's name and title for this message.

7. This letter should be addressed to:

   Dr. Jarilyn J. Garber, treasurer
   First Federal, Inc.
   Stanford Building
   Baton Rouge, LA 70893

8. The raw materials for our major product are grown in the west.

9. The report was submitted by ex-president Jones.

10. Turn east on Elm to reach our offices in West Memphis.

▤ EXERCISE

Complete the exercise below to check your ability to proofread material containing a variety of capitalization errors. Use revision marks to indicate errors. Rewrite or retype this material on another page. Be sure to proofread your final copy.

MINUTES OF QUARTERLY MEETING

The quarterly meeting was held in Roanoke on Monday, November 7. The meeting was called to order by President-Elect Carpenter. Members attended from many states, including Kentucky, Michigan, New york, Florida, and south Carolina.

The minutes were read by Gerald Longe, Secretary of the firm. Lois Dapplewhite presented the Treasurer's report. These Reports were approved.

Discussion was held concerning the purchase of new equipment. Presentations were made by representatives of Campbell Equipment company, Shroeder & Sons Equipment, and Rhodes equipment. A final decision will be made at the next meeting.

The next quarterly meeting will be held in west Palm Beach, Florida, in february.

Gerald Longe, secretary

▤ EXERCISE 5.7

Complete the exercise below to check your ability to proofread material containing a variety of capitalization errors. Use revision marks to indicate errors. Rewrite or retype this material on another page. Be sure to proofread your final copy.

MEMORANDUM

TO: Danielle K. Willey, Office systems department

FROM: William F. Byerly, personnel director

DATE: February 2, 19--

SUBJECT: personnel forms

Please complete the attached personnel forms and return them to Joanna Willingham, secretary to mr. Larrabee in the personnel office downtown. These forms must be completed and returned by Friday, February 5, for your personnel records to be complete. Once your records are in order, you will be eligible to take off Holidays with pay.

We do not close our offices for Valentine's day. Our next holiday will be in March.

rt

▤ EXERCISE   5.8

Complete the exercise below to check your ability to proofread material containing a variety of capitalization errors. Use revision marks to indicate errors. Rewrite or retype this material on another page. Be sure to proofread your final copy.

MEMORANDUM

TO: Clarke Weston, Travel Department

FROM: R. j. King, manager

DATE: December 7, 19--

SUBJECT: Travel itinerary

Please make reservations for my trip next week. I plan to leave on Monday, December 13, and go to New York. I would like a Flight in the early morning, if possible. I would prefer to stay at the Randolph Towers. I will be meeting with staff members of McPherson company.

I plan to leave New york on Thursday and travel to Minneapolis. I will not be able to leave New York before Noon. I would prefer to stay at the Hardison Hotel in minneapolis, as it is close to my meeting at the Donaldson Company headquarters. I need to return home on Friday Night.

I will not need reservations for ground transportation. Transportation will be provided by the Companies I am visiting.

gd

▤ EXERCISE   5.9

Complete the exercise below to check your ability to proofread material containing a variety of capitalization errors. Use revision marks to indicate errors. Rewrite or retype this material on another page. Be sure to proofread your final copy.

january 5, 19--

Mr. Bernard Osteranski
Training Director
Irwin Industries
Cincinnati, OH 45215-1453

Dear mr. Osteranski

Thank you for inviting me to speak to your supervisors about our employee induction program. We feel we have a very successful program and are pleased that Irwin industries is interested.

I would like to be able to come to your annual meeting and explain our system; however, I have already scheduled another meeting for February 2. If you could schedule your meeting for another date that did not conflict with my schedule, I would be happy to come to cincinnati to talk with your Supervisors.

Sincerely Yours

Mitchell Kingsbury
Employee relations

ft

📋 EXERCISE   5.10

Complete the exercise below to check your ability to proofread material containing a variety of capitalization errors. Use revision marks to indicate errors. Rewrite or retype this material on another page. Be sure to proofread your final copy.

USE OF ELECTRONIC MAIL

The purpose of this report is to determine the potential use of electronic mail for United Technologies, inc.   This report was authorized by president Albert Nanney.

Several of our competitors have begun using forms of electronic mail to increase the speed of communication to customers.   Among those now using some form of electronic mail are Franklin industries, Davenport and Jackson, Inc., and Lloyd brothers, Inc.

Our Study has shown that it would be beneficial to use facsimile equipment to send Documents more quickly between our main office and the branches in Albuquerque, Pueblo, and Santa fe.   The cost of the service would be less than the potential increase in Sales.

The remainder of this report will include a description of the features of each system available and the Cost considerations.

Chapter

USE OF ABBREVIATIONS

What's Wrong Here?

Seen on a sign in a bank: The baby weighed 8′ 12 oz.

When you use abbreviations, you must be sure that they are standard so that the receiver will understand and interpret them correctly. In addition, several capitalization and punctuation decisions must be made.

Abbreviations are classified as informal writing and should be used only when appropriate for the situation. Ordinary words are not usually abbreviated in business messages. When in doubt, follow the custom of the organization, consult a reference book, or spell out the word. ■

Since abbreviations often have very few letters, they must be proofread *very* carefully. A one-letter mistake can cause serious problems. For example, if Memphis, TN, were changed to Memphis, TX, a letter could be sent to the wrong state. If a 2 p.m. meeting time were typed as 2 a.m., many people could be inconvenienced.

Follow these guidelines in using abbreviations:

1. Abbreviate and capitalize seniority titles, references to academic degrees, and professional designations when used following a person's name. Use a comma before *and after* the abbreviation when it appears in the middle of a sentence. Most abbreviations of this type are separated by periods. Exceptions include CPA (Certified Public Accountant) and CPS (Certified Professional Secretary).

   > Our new training director is Daphne Latham, Ph.D.
   > John Williamson, Sr., will be arriving at our plant June 10.
   > Jerry Ann Darling, CPA, is our new internal auditor.

2. Abbreviate and capitalize the names of business, professional, and other organizations commonly recognized by their initials. No periods are used within the abbreviations.

> FBI   (Federal Bureau of Investigation)
> IRS   (Internal Revenue Service)
> IBM (International Business Machines)

RELATED ASSIGNMENT:	EXERCISE 6.1, PAGE 89
	EXERCISE 6.2, PAGE 90

3. Abbreviate parts of a firm's name only if abbreviated in the official name of the organization.

> Jones Bros. Hardware is one of our customers.
> Clarke Corporation will be sending us its latest brochure.
> Superstation, Inc., has a new product of interest to us.

4. Abbreviate time zones (Eastern Standard Time, Central Daylight Time, etc.) using capital letters and no periods within the abbreviation; abbreviate the time designations, a.m. and p.m., with lowercase letters and periods.

> Mr. Frank Walker will be presenting his talk in Boston Friday at 8 p.m., EST.

RELATED ASSIGNMENT:	EXERCISE 6.3, PAGE 91
	EXERCISE 6.4, PAGE 92

5. Abbreviate units of measure when space is limited, which often occurs when completing business forms such as invoices. Use a period after one-word abbreviations but no period after abbreviations of more than one word.

> 12 ft. (12 feet)   100 wpm (100 words per minute)

6. Abbreviate names of states, especially in addresses, using the two-letter state abbreviations. Both letters are capitalized and no period is used. Separate the state abbreviation from the ZIP Code by one or two spaces.

> Mr. Logan Washington
> 2500 Bellevue
> Elk City, OK 73644

7. Plural forms of abbreviations are often formed by adding a lowercase *s* to singular abbreviations; no apostrophe is needed.

> Plural form of CPA = CPAs

A list of commonly abbreviated names and terms is given on page 85. The two-letter state abbreviations are shown on page 87.

RELATED ASSIGNMENT:	EXERCISE 6.5, PAGE 93
	EXERCISE 6.6, PAGE 94

END-OF-CHAPTER ASSIGNMENT:	EXERCISES 6.7 THROUGH 6.10, PAGES 95 THROUGH 98.

COMMONLY USED ABBREVIATIONS

Personal Titles and Business Names

Jr.	Junior
Sr.	Senior
M.D.	Doctor of Medicine
Ph.D.	Doctor of Philosophy
CPA	Certified Public Accountant
CPS	Certified Professional Secretary
CLU	Chartered Life Underwriter
Ed.D.	Doctor of Education
B.A.	Bachelor of Arts
M.B.A.	Master of Business Administration
Corp.	Corporation
Co.	Company
Inc.	Incorporated
Ltd.	Limited

Organization Names

AAA	American Automobile Association
FCC	Federal Communications Commission
UN	United Nations
IBM	International Business Machines
GM	General Motors
NASA	National Aeronautics and Space Administration
FBI	Federal Bureau of Investigation
IRS	Internal Revenue Service
BBB	Better Business Bureau
FDIC	Federal Deposit Insurance Corporation
HUD	Housing and Urban Development
NLRB	National Labor Relations Board
SEC	Securities and Exchange Commission
TVA	Tennessee Valley Authority
VA	Veterans' Administration
AMA	American Medical Association

Business Terms

No.	Number
c.o.d.	cash on delivery
f.o.b.	free on board
MBO	management by objectives
acct.	account
LIFO	last in, first out
FIFO	first in, first out
mgr.	manager
mdse.	merchandise
UPC	Universal Product Code
c/o	in care of
cr.	credit, creditor
dr.	debit
mfg.	manufacturing
pp.	pages
e.g.	(foreign term) for example
i.e.	(foreign term) that is
et al.	(foreign term) and others
etc.	(foreign term) and so forth
std.	standard
misc.	miscellaneous
ASAP	as soon as possible

Units of Measure

ft.	foot
in.	inch
lb.	pound
oz.	ounce
wpm	words per minute
mph	miles per hour
m	meter
g	gram
l	liter
cm	centimeter
kg	kilogram
km	kilometer
C	Centigrade
F	Fahrenheit
pt.	pint
qt.	quart
mm	millimeter
sq. in.	square inch
ht.	height
wt.	weight
doz.	dozen

Time References

hr.	hour
min.	minute
sec.	second
yr.	year
mo.	month
EST	Eastern Standard Time
CST	Central Standard Time
MST	Mountain Standard Time
PST	Pacific Standard Time
EDT	Eastern Daylight Time
CDT	Central Daylight Time
MDT	Mountain Daylight Time
PDT	Pacific Daylight Time

Addresses

St.	Street
Ave.	Avenue
Blvd.	Boulevard
Rd.	Road

TWO-LETTER ABBREVIATIONS OF STATES, TERRITORIES, AND PROVINCES

State Name	Abbreviation	State Name	Abbreviation
Alabama	AL	Montana	MT
Alaska	AK	Nebraska	NE
Arizona	AZ	Nevada	NV
Arkansas	AR	New Hampshire	NH
California	CA	New Jersey	NJ
Colorado	CO	New Mexico	NM
Connecticut	CT	New York	NY
Delaware	DE	North Carolina	NC
Florida	FL	North Dakota	ND
Georgia	GA	Ohio	OH
Hawaii	HI	Oklahoma	OK
Idaho	ID	Oregon	OR
Illinois	IL	Pennsylvania	PA
Indiana	IN	Rhode Island	RI
Iowa	IA	South Carolina	SC
Kansas	KS	South Dakota	SD
Kentucky	KY	Tennessee	TN
Louisiana	LA	Texas	TX
Maine	ME	Utah	UT
Maryland	MD	Vermont	VT
Massachusetts	MA	Virginia	VA
Michigan	MI	Washington	WA
Minnesota	MN	West Virginia	WV
Mississippi	MS	Wisconsin	WI
Missouri	MO	Wyoming	WY

District/Territory Name — Abbreviations

District/Territory Name	Abbreviations
District of Columbia	DC
Guam	GU
Puerto Rico	PR
Virgin Islands	VI

Canadian Provinces

Alberta	AB
British Columbia	BC
Labrador	LB
Manitoba	MB
New Brunswick	NB
Newfoundland	NF
Northwest Territories	NT
Nova Scotia	NS
Ontario	ON
Prince Edward Island	PE
Quebec	PQ
Saskatchewan	SK
Yukon Territory	YT

📋 EXERCISE 6.1

Complete the exercise below to practice proofreading abbreviations and related capitalization and punctuation. Use revision marks to indicate changes needed on the typed copy. Some errors could have occurred in the handwritten copy which *may* have been corrected on the typed copy.

1. *The new director of word processing services is Clarice Chandler, c.p.s.*

   The new director of word processing services is Clarice Chandler, CPA.

2. *We are considering buying some I.B.M. equipment.*

   We are considering buying some IBM equipment.

3. *Sean Robertson, jr., is our new employee in marketing research.*

   Sean Robertson, Jr. is our new employee in marketing research.

4. *We will meet with Agnes Goldstein, M.D., at 3 pm.*

   We will meet with Agnes Goldstein M.D., at 3 a.m.

5. *Angela Mapley, CPA, will be investigated by the FBI and IRS.*

   Angela Mapley, CPA, will be investigated by the FBI and IRA.

📋 EXERCISE

Complete the exercise below to practice proofreading abbreviations and related capitalization and punctuation. Use revision marks to indicate changes needed on the typed copy. Some errors could have occurred in the handwritten copy which *may* have been corrected on the typed copy.

We will be conducting our yearly progress review meeting on Fri., Jan. 40, at 4 p.m., in the conference room. Our research director, John Lowry, Phd. will conduct the meeting. Minutes will be taken by Gerald Morgan, cps. Awards will be presented by Bruce Coleman, Sr.

We will be conducting our yearly progress review meeting on Friday, January 10, at 4 p.m, in the conference room. Our research director, John Lowry, Ph.D. will conduct the meeting. Minutes will be taken by Gerald Morgan, c.p.s. Awards will be presented by Bruce Coleman, sr.

📄 EXERCISE   6.3

Complete the exercise below to practice proofreading abbreviations and related capitalization and punctuation. Use revision marks to indicate changes needed on the typed copy. Some errors could have occurred in the handwritten copy which *may* have been corrected on the typed copy.

1. *On my recent flight, I left Atlanta at 8 a.m., E.S.T., and arrived in Memphis at 8 a.m., C.S.T.*

On my recent flight, I left Atlanta at 8 a.m., EST, and arrived in Memphis at 8 a.m., EST.

2. *Please send a copy of this memo to Mr. F. D'Angelis, Jr., in Littleton, CO.*

Please send a copy of this memo to Mr. F. D'Angelis, Sr. in Littleton, CO.

3. *Jamison, Inc., will be expanding its business by adding a branch office in Portland, OR.*

Jamison, Inc. will be expanding its business by adding a branch office in Portland, OR.

4. *Watch for differences in time zones; what time is it in Boston when it is 3 p.m, MDT?*

Watch for differences in time zones; what time is it in Boston when it is 3 p.m., MDT?

5. *Mason Bros. is opening a display on some blvd. in the downtown area.*

Mason Bros. is opening a display on some blvd. in the downtown area.

▤ EXERCISE   6.4

Complete the exercise below to practice proofreading abbreviations and related capitalization and
punctuation. Use revision marks to indicate changes needed on the typed copy.

All caps → [Time Zones for Major Cities We Serve

Alphabetize {

Boston	E.S.T.
Tulsa	C.S.T.
Amarillo	C.S.T.
Denver	M.S.T.
Miami	E.S.T.
Sacramento	P.S.T.

TIME ZONES FOR MAJOR CITIES WE SERVE

Amarillo	e.s.t.
Boston	c.s.t.
Denver	c.s.t.
Miami	m.s.t.
Sacramento	e.s.t.
Tulsa	p.s.t.

🗐 EXERCISE

Complete the exercise below to practice proofreading abbreviations and related capitalization and punctuation. Use revision marks to indicate changes needed on the typed copy.

MEMORANDUM

TO: Purchasing Dept.
FROM: Joe Daily, Maintenance
DATE: 9/3/--
SUBJECT: Items Needed for Maintenance

Please order the following mdse, preferably from Lincoln Mfg., Chattanooga, Tn.:

    12 qts.   transmission fluid
    1 case   8-oz. containers, rubber cement

Please ask them to put this on our acct.

MEMORANDUM

TO: Purchasing Department

FROM: Joe Daily, Maintenance

DATE: September 3, 19--

SUBJECT: Items Needed for Maintenance

Please order the following merchandise, preferably from Lincoln Manufacturing, Chattanooga, Tn.:

    12 pts.   transmission fluid

    1 case   8-lb. containers, rubber cement

Please ask them to put this on our acct.

jt

NAME

▤ EXERCISE   6.6

Complete the exercise below to practice proofreading abbreviations and related capitalization and punctuation. Use revision marks to indicate changes needed. Assume that the figures given are correct.

MEMORANDUM

TO: Claire DuBois, Personnel Director

FROM: Julia Lambe, Testing

DATE: November 28, 19--

SUBJECT: Typing Test Results

Here are the results of the typing test given to applicants for the secretarial position in the engineering division:

Loretta Maester	50 w.p.m.
Bobbie Klampton	47 w.p.m.
Terrance Carson, Jr.	53 w.p.m.
Maxine Dean	71 w.p.m.

bl

▤ EXERCISE

Complete the exercise below to practice proofreading abbreviations and related capitalization and punctuation. Use revision marks to indicate changes needed in the typed copy.

MEMORANDUM

TO: All Employees

FROM: Roy E. Dobkins, Mgr.

DATE: Dec. 12, 19--

SUBJECT: Working Hours

Here are the new opening and closing times for some of our offices:

Cleveland, OK   8:15 a.m. – 5:15 p.m.   C.S.T.
Seattle, WA   9:00 a.m. – 5:30 p.m.   P.S.T.
Kansas City, KS 8:30 a.m. – 4:30 p.m.   C.S.T.
Knoxville, TN   8:30 a.m. – 5:30 p.m.   E.S.T.
Tucumcari, NM   8:00 a.m.– 5:00 p.m.   M.S.T.

Please keep these times in mind when calling these offices.

MEMORANDUM

TO: All Employees

FROM: Roy E. Dobkins, Manager

DATE: December 12, 19--

SUBJECT: Working Hours

Here are the new opening and closing times for some of our offices:

Cleveland, OH	8:15 a.m.–5:15 p.m.	CST
Seattle, WA	9:00 a.m.–5:30 p.m.	PST
Kansas City, KS	8:30 a.m.–4:30 p.m.	CST
Knoxville, TN	8:30 a.m.–5:30 p.m.	EST
Tucumcari, MN	8:30 a.m.–5:00 p.m.	MST

Please keep these times in mind when calling these offices.

js

📃 EXERCISE   6.8

Complete the exercise below to practice proofreading abbreviations and related capitalization and punctuation. Use revision marks to indicate changes needed.

MEMORANDUM

TO: Grant Johnson, Sr., Engineering

FROM: Willard Skoog, Personnel

DATE: March 31, 19--

SUBJECT: Applicant for Position

Raymond K Derryberry, Edd. will be visiting our offices on Monday. He is interested in a position as an engineer in your department. He has worked for the past five years for N.A.S.A. His other experience as an engineer was with Tva, where he worked for seven yrs.

Please arrange for several of the staff members to be available to have lunch with Mr. Derryberry at 1 a.m. Monday. He will be here from 9 a.m. until 4:30 p.m.

gg

▤ EXERCISE   **6.9**

Complete the exercise below to practice proofreading abbreviations and related capitalization and punctuation. Use revision marks to indicate changes needed.

MEMORANDUM

TO: Freeman Winston, Word Processing

FROM: James Ziemer, Manager

DATE: July 1, 19--

SUBJECT: Reports and Other Documents

Please have the attached materials typed for me as soon as you can.

Several additional pp. of materials will be coming from Marla Prather, mgr. of the Atlanta office.   These materials include letters, reports, ect.

We will need a cc of each item sent to Wilson Watson, jr.

fk

▤ EXERCISE 6.10

Complete the exercise below to practice proofreading abbreviations and related capitalization and punctuation. Use revision marks to indicate changes needed.

February 28, 19--

Dr. Amy Lutz
Rayburn and Taylor, Inc.
4754 Norway Bvld.
Scranton, PA 15230

Dear Mr. Lutz

Thank you for your help in our recent search for a new external accountant. At your suggestion, we have talked with Glen Daughtrey CPA, about our financial needs. He has experience working with S.E.C. matters and has been very helpful to us.

We are talking with the other person you recommended, Arthur Pyun, PhD., next week. We will be meeting him in Galveston, TX on Wednesday. His experience working with U.P.C. should help us with our packaging and labeling decisions.

Sincerely

Lydia Zysk, Manager

kk

Chapter

WORD USAGE

What's Wrong Here?

Written in a memo: Do not forget you're computer software.

One of the most common proofreading problems is finding a correctly spelled word that is incorrectly used. Many words sound alike or almost alike but have different meanings. Errors in word usage are more difficult to find than many other kinds of mistakes. Word processing equipment with spelling checker programs cannot even detect such errors. Therefore, sentences must be read for content and meaning with close attention to each word.

Contractions, shortened forms of words, often sound very much like other words. An apostrophe is used in a contraction to show where letters have been left out. To proofread contractions, read the sentence as if the long forms of the words were included. If the material does not make sense, the wrong word was probably used.

The use of contractions is recommended only for very informal writing and for business forms with limited space. Generally, you should avoid using contractions in business writing. ■

In this chapter you will study words that are often misused. Becoming more aware of specific words to watch for will be helpful as you develop your proofreading skill. Similar sounding words, along with brief definitions, are listed below. Consult a dictionary for more detailed explanations of the meanings and uses of each word.

■ SIMILAR SOUNDING WORDS

| 1. | accede (agree) | We will <u>accede</u> to your request. |
| | exceed (surpass) | Do not <u>exceed</u> the spending limit when you travel. |

99

2. accept (receive)   Please accept our deposit.
   except (exclude)   Everyone except Joshua was at work today.

3. access (admittance)   You must have a card to gain access to the computer room.
   excess (surplus)   We have excess funds in our supplies budget.

4. ad (advertisement)   Our ad is in this morning's newspaper.
   add (increase)   We need to add four more chairs in the meeting room.

5. adapt (adjust)   We can adapt our procedures to this change.
   adept (skilled)   Lawrence is adept at handling grievances.
   adopt (choose; approve) We will adopt a new format for our annual reports.

6. addition (increase)   Four graphs are enclosed in addition to the tables.
   edition (published form) The latest edition of our report will be ready today.

7. advice (recommendation)   Please consider my advice.
   advise (to recommend -verb) I would advise you to study the manual carefully.

8. affect (influence)   How will the legislation affect our office?
   effect (to accomplish -verb; We will effect a compromise; we will study the effect.
   result -noun)

9. aid (help)   The Red Cross will aid victims of disasters.
                       Norman will aid you in finishing the project.
   aide (helper)   Logan served as an aide to the chairman.

10. allowed (permitted)   Rita was allowed to take her vacation this week.
    aloud (out loud)   The minutes of the meeting were read aloud.

RELATED ASSIGNMENT: **EXERCISE 7.1, PAGE 107**

---

11. all ready (prepared)   We are all ready for the monthly meeting.
    already (beforehand)   The meeting agenda has already been prepared.

12.	all right (satisfactory) alright	It is all right for relatives to tour the plant today. (never appropriate in business writing)
13.	allude (refer to) elude (escape)	He may allude to his previous report. He was able to elude his followers.
14.	any one (any thing in a group) anyone (any person)	Please submit any one of your proposals. Anyone who needs transportation should call me.
15.	any way (any method) anyway (in any case)	I do not believe there is any way to finish early. We will work until closing time anyway.
16.	ascent (rise) assent (agreement)	I was impressed with his quick ascent to the top. All members gave their assent to the plan.
17.	assistance (help) assistants (helpers)	I would appreciate your assistance with this job. Two new assistants will start work next month.
18.	attendance (people present) attendants (assistants)	How many were in attendance? The three parking attendants were kept busy.
19.	berth (space; bed) birth (beginning)	John reserved a berth on the ship. Our forefathers gave birth to a new nation.
20.	beside (at the side of) besides (in addition to)	The work area was located beside the main desk. Three departments besides Accounting met the deadline.

RELATED ASSIGNMENT: **EXERCISE 7.2,   PAGE 108**

21.	biannual (twice a year) biennial (every two years)	The biannual meeting of stockholders was held today. The biennial visit from the president will occur Friday.
22.	capital (money; seat of government) capitol (building)	Considerable capital has been invested in the project. A tour of the capitol will be included in the trip.

23. cite (quote; summon)   You should cite several references in the document.
    sight (vision; aim)   His sight was limited by the darkness.
    site (location)   A decision was made today about the new plant site.

24. coarse (rough)   Our new product has a coarse texture.
    course   What course should we follow?
    (route; direction; school
    unit)

25. complement   The new carpeting will complement the current office
    (to complete; to make   decor.
    perfect -verb)

    compliment   I appreciate your compliment regarding my work.
    (praise -noun;
    to praise -verb)

26. cooperation (joint action)   We would appreciate your cooperation.
    corporation   Jack, Mark, and Leon recently formed a corporation.
    (type of business)

27. correspondence   Our correspondence with customers has been improving.
    (written messages)

    correspondents   The newspaper contacted its correspondents in our area.
    (writers; reporters)

28. council (governing body)   The proposal was given to the joint council.
    counsel (advice)   Lois Davis serves as our legal counsel.

29. credible (believable)   She gave a credible explanation for the delay.
    creditable (praiseworthy)   The suggestion submitted by Mr. Samuels was creditable.

30. desert (abandon)   Do not desert us until we finish the job.
    dessert (food)   The banquet dessert was chocolate mousse.

RELATED ASSIGNMENT: EXERCISE 7.3,   PAGE 109

---

31. disburse (pay out)   We will disburse payroll checks at 3 p.m.
    disperse (scatter)   After the participants disperse, we will study the results.

32. eminent (prominent)   Our new department head is an <u>eminent</u> authority on task analysis.

    imminent (about to occur)   Our employees are in no <u>imminent</u> danger.

33. every day (each day)   Please report your progress to me <u>every day</u>.

    everyday (ordinary)   Repairs are an <u>everyday</u> occurrence in the plant.

34. farther (greater distance)   Dorothy has <u>farther</u> to travel than the others.

    further (additional)   Please read the manual for <u>further</u> instructions.

35. fiscal (financial)   Our <u>fiscal</u> year begins on July 1.

    physical   Employee morale can be affected by <u>physical</u> surroundings.
    (material; of the body)

36. incidence (occurrence)   Please report any <u>incidence</u> of tardiness.

    incidents (events)   Several important <u>incidents</u> occurred this week.

37. incite (rouse)   He hoped to <u>incite</u> some action from the crowd.

    insight (wisdom)   Her <u>insight</u> was very helpful during the meeting.

38. it's (contraction of <u>it is</u>)   <u>It's</u> going to be interesting when we change systems.

    its (possessive form of <u>it</u>)   Their company should change <u>its</u> hiring practices.

39. leased (rented)   We have <u>leased</u> ten new microcomputers.

    least (smallest)   James will complete at <u>least</u> six copies today.

40. loose (not tight)   <u>Loose</u> wiring caused the printer to quit working.

    lose (misplace)   Be careful not to <u>lose</u> your copy of the changes.

┌───┐
│   **RELATED ASSIGNMENT:**   **EXERCISE 7.4,   PAGE 110**   │
└───┘

41. moral (ethical)   We need to use <u>moral</u> considerations in making decisions.

    morale (mental condition)   Employee <u>morale</u> about this project is good.

42. principal   The <u>principal</u> on our loan is $50,000.
    (capital; sum; chief)

    principle (rule; truth)   The <u>principle</u> of equal treatment is involved.

43. quiet (noiseless)   Our new equipment is quiet.
    quite (entirely)   Miranda's work is quite good.

44. raise (elevate; increase)   We need to raise our level of productivity.
    raze (demolish)   We have decided to raze the old building.

45. sale   Our old equipment will be for sale at a good price.
    (process of selling -noun)
    sell (to exchange -verb)   We sell all our old typewriters.

46. some time (period of time)   It will take some time before our new offices are ready.
    sometime (indefinite time)   We plan to move sometime in May.

47. stationary (not moving)   Our new office will have very few stationary walls.
    stationery (writing paper)   Please use the appropriate stationery when writing to
                                 customers.

48. their   All employees have been asked to complete their weekly
    (possessive form of they)   assignments on time.
    there (in that place)   All research personnel will be there.
    they're   They're having a party during the holiday season.
    (contraction of they are)

49. who's   Who's responsible for checking the budget figures?
    (contraction of who is)
    whose   Whose equipment provides the nicest appearing letters?
    (possessive form of who)

50. your   Please bring your notes with you when you come.
    (possessive form of you)
    you're   You're expected to participate in the discussion.
    (contraction of you are)

RELATED ASSIGNMENT: EXERCISE 7.5,   PAGE 111

■ Other Frequently Misused Words

among   The materials will be distributed among the five workers.
(more than two persons/things)

between   He must choose between the two people for the new
(two persons/things)   position.

amount (mass items; singular nouns)	The <u>amount</u> of time spent was substantial.
number (countable items; plural nouns)	The <u>number</u> of pages in the report was seven.
as (used as a conjunction in a clause)	<u>As</u> I said last week, paychecks will be early this month.
like (used as a preposition)	There are not enough employees <u>like</u> him.
choose (select)	We will <u>choose</u> new officers at the next meeting.
chose (past tense of choose)	He <u>chose</u> his new office furniture last week.
continual (occurring regularly)	The <u>continual</u> breakdowns on the equipment are hurting production.
continuous (uninterrupted)	Our data processing equipment is available on a 24-hour, <u>continuous</u> basis.
fewer (countable items; plural nouns)	We had <u>fewer</u> problems with absenteeism last month.
less (mass items; singular noun)	It took <u>less</u> time than expected to finish the work.
I (used as a subject)	Sheila and <u>I</u> will take care of the arrangements.
me (used as an object)	Between you and <u>me</u>, the work will get finished on time.
imply (suggest)	The message seems to <u>imply</u> that a change is needed.
infer (reach a conclusion)	You can <u>infer</u> from the results that we have succeeded.
interstate (between states)	Our newest <u>interstate</u> route includes Kentucky and Missouri.
intrastate (within a state)	We are considering a new <u>intrastate</u> telephone service.
precede (go before)	A summary of the results will <u>precede</u> the details.
proceed (continue)	Please <u>proceed</u> with the planned improvements.

RELATED ASSIGNMENT:	**EXERCISE 7.6, PAGE 112**

END-OF-CHAPTER ASSIGNMENT:	**EXERCISES 7.7 THROUGH 7.10, PAGES 113 THROUGH 116**

▤ EXERCISE

Complete the exercise below to improve your skill in correct word usage. Circle the correct word in each sentence below.

1. I need your (advice, advise) on these recommendations.

2. The enclosed reference manual should (aid, aide) you as you complete your work.

3. We would be pleased if you would (accept, except) the position as treasurer of the organization.

4. The clerical employees in our office will be (allowed, aloud) to change their lunch time next week.

5. We must (adapt, adept, adopt) our facilities to meet the new safety requirements.

6. Actual production has (acceded, exceeded) our expectations.

7. Very few of our employees have (access, excess) to the vault.

8. If we raise the price of our product, what will be the (affect, effect) on our sales volume?

9. The tenth (addition, edition) of our annual reports will be published next week.

10. Please (ad, add) three brochures to the letter being sent to Mr. Davis.

▤ EXERCISE

Complete the exercise below to practice proofreading for correct word usage. Use revision marks to indicate any corrections needed.

1. Is there anyway to get the project finished by Friday?

2. Anyone of these applicants would be acceptable for the position.

3. The success of our latest product has given birth to a new product idea.

4. Most of the responses to the questionnaire have all ready been received.

5. For the annual company picture, please stand besides the statue of our founder.

6. His ascent up the company "ladder" has been rapid.

7. Will it be all right for Cecilia to be 30 minutes late tomorrow?

8. Staff attendants at the meeting is required.

9. Your three assistance will be needed this afternoon.

10. I eluded to that concept in my earlier letter.

▤ EXERCISE

Complete the exercise below to practice proofreading for correct word usage. Use revision marks to indicate any corrections needed.

1. We sighted several problems while visiting the cite of our new office building.

2. Supervisors should complement their employees' work whenever appropriate.

3. I have suggested that our sales department seek help from the advertising counsel.

4. Our retiring vice president has promised not to dessert us before the end of the project.

5. The biannual meeting of the long-range planning committee is today; several changes have occurred since the last meeting two years ago.

6. The reason Alan gave for his lack of progress was creditable.

7. We certainly appreciated your corporation on our recent project.

8. Our word processing office has eight correspondence secretaries.

9. How much capitol would be required for the proposed expansion?

10. A new type of course material will be used on the office walls.

🖩 EXERCISE 7.4

Complete the exercise below to practice proofreading for correct word usage. Use revision marks to indicate any corrections needed.

1. The accounting department will have the annual physical reports on the company's financial status completed by Monday.

2. Your insight was certainly appreciated in the meeting today.

3. Your time records must be turned in everyday.

4. We had a large turnout for our credit union meeting, but the crowd has now disbursed.

5. You will not be able to enter the building if you loose your identification card.

6. Our research department will be visited today by Gordon James, the imminent scientist.

7. Every department is responsible for it's own records.

8. How much farther will our sales team travel this year?

9. The temporary equipment will be leased for two months.

10. Several unusual incidence occurred last week.

🗒 EXERCISE   7.5

Complete the exercise below to practice proofreading for correct word usage. Use revision marks to indicate any corrections needed.

1.   Employee salaries will be razed by September.

2.   All persons must bring their own repair tools.

3.   A pay raise is expected to help improve employee moral.

4.   Our new stationary will be used for all outside correspondence.

5.   We would like to sale some of our old furniture.

6.   Your going to be pleased with the new arrangement of the office furniture.

7.   The principle reason for our change in policies was for increased sales.

8.   She is the person who's job is being upgraded next month.

9.   The change in ownership occurred some time last year.

10.   The materials received from data processing were not quite complete.

▤ EXERCISE   7.6

Complete the exercise below to practice proofreading for correct word usage. Use revision marks to indicate any corrections needed.

1. What amount of money is needed to complete the project?

2. We choose new officers at last month's meeting.

3. An equipment demonstration will be presented today for you and I.

4. Please distribute the supplies between the three typists in your office.

5. Our plant had less accidents this year than last year.

6. Our intrastate service includes the cities of Dallas, Tulsa, and Kansas City.

7. We will proceed with the construction project next week.

8. Like I said, the trainees will be arriving Monday.

9. The memo inferred that we would be receiving an additional fringe benefit next year.

10. The receptionist has difficulty getting much clerical work done because of the continual telephone calls.

▤ EXERCISE 7.7

Complete the exercise below to practice proofreading for correct word usage. Use revision marks to indicate any corrections needed. Rewrite or retype the paragraph in the space provided at the bottom of the page. Be sure to proofread your final copy.

```
     We would appreciate your cooperation in our project to
improve our letter and memo correspondents.  We are asking for
your assistants in determining if we have excess wording.  We
will also try to learn if our messages have the affect we want.
We plan to study all written messages accept reports.
     Please keep records of your writing activities every day;
then give us your advise on what amount of changes we should
make in our procedures.
```

▤ EXERCISE   7.8

Complete the exercise below to practice proofreading for correct word usage. Use revision marks to indicate any corrections needed.

MEMORANDUM

TO: Vance Byrd, Head Mechanic

FROM: Lola Barnes, Insurance Department

DATE: May 31, 19--

SUBJECT: Losses in Fire

What amount of tools was stored in the tool building that burned? Knowing this information should help Darren and I make our final report. We do not want to loose any money by not having correct information.

We will need your final statement of losses some time next week. You're assistants in this matter is appreciated.

kf

▤ EXERCISE

Complete the exercise below to practice proofreading for correct word usage. Use revision marks to indicate any corrections needed.

MEMORANDUM

TO: Daphne Vanlandenburg, Advertising

FROM: Jo-Etta Menske, Public Relations

DATE: October 20, 19--

SUBJECT: Opening of New Retail Store

Please place an add in the local newspaper announcing the November 2 opening of our new retail store. The ad should mention that this store is in edition to our other three stores all ready located in this area. The store is located on the cite of the old capitol. The ad should also state that there is easy access to it's parking lot from the Park Avenue entrance.

We are quiet pleased to be opening this store and look forward to serving our customers in this area everyday.

lp

▤ EXERCISE 7.10

Complete the exercise below to practice proofreading for correct word usage. Use revision marks to indicate any corrections needed.

March 12, 19--

Mr. Matt Clark
624 Jasper
Juneau, AK 99801

Dear Mr. Clark

Thank you for your letter inquiring about working in our Chicago office. We are pleased that your interested in working for us.

We are currently looking for new employees in the areas of engineering and accounting but are not able to hire persons in areas beside those. We would normally be interested in hiring any one with qualifications as good as yours but are not allowed to at this time. As soon as it is alright for us to hire in additional areas, we will contact you. However, I have been told that it may be some time before we can make farther changes in our staff.

We appreciate your understanding and cooperation. If there were anyway to consider hiring you soon, we would certainly be happy to set up an appointment to talk with you.

Sincerely

Luther Nacke
Personnel Director

yt

Chapter

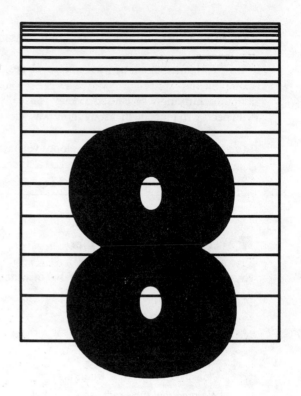

CLARITY, CONCISENESS, AND OTHER CONTENT CONSIDERATIONS

❓ What's Wrong Here?

Printed in a letter: Please contact this desk if you have any questions.

Messages should be clear, correct, and concise. Your job as a good proofreader includes editing when necessary to improve the clarity of the message. A confusing message wastes the reader's time and may not be read. Be sure the author is willing to accept your suggestions before you make any major changes in the wording. You must be careful, of course, not to change the meaning of the message. As stated earlier, if you are not sure of the meaning, consult the author.

■ UNNECESSARY INFORMATION

Sometimes the information that is presented is obvious and should be left out. In other cases, the information is repeated unnecessarily. You should edit these sentences to shorten them.

A shorter sentence and shorter message will often be clearer simply because fewer words have to be read and understood. However, messages should not be so short that important information is left out. ■

Examples of an unnecessary sentence at the beginning of a letter are:

This letter is in reply to your letter.

—or—

We have received your letter.

Obviously, we would not be answering the letter if we had not received it.

Sometimes information that is unnecessary is also negative in tone. For example:

You failed to tell us what size envelopes you need; please send us this information.

Identifying who caused a delay is usually unnecessary; simply asking for the information you need will indicate that something was left out of the previous message.

Please tell us what size envelopes you need.

RELATED ASSIGNMENT:	EXERCISE 8.1, PAGE 121

■ REDUNDANCIES

Redundancies are word combinations in which the thought is expressed twice. Here are some examples:

Redundancy	Correct Usage
I first began working here three years ago.	I began working here three years ago.
Please repeat your instructions again.	Please repeat your instructions.
We received the exact same memo last week.	We received the same memo last week.
Please refer back to my report of April 2 for more information.	Please refer to my report of April 2 for more information.
My past experience includes a year as a correspondence secretary in a word processing center.	My experience includes a year as a correspondence secretary in a word processing center.

Redundant wording should be edited to eliminate unnecessary words.

RELATED ASSIGNMENT:	EXERCISE 8.2, PAGE 122

■ OTHER WORDY EXPRESSIONS

Sometimes expressions are used out of habit, and the author may not realize that the message is becoming cluttered and harder to understand. The trend in writing is to shorten long, wordy phrases, especially those that sound old-fashioned or insincere. Some examples of this wording are:

Wordy or Old-fashioned	Recommended Wording
Please be advised that your monthly report is due Friday.	Your monthly report is due Friday.
Enclosed please find a copy of our latest financial statement.	Enclosed is a copy of our latest financial statement.
Our next regional meeting will be held in the city of Austin.	Our next regional meeting will be held in Austin.

Our reports will be a week late <u>in view of the fact that</u> necessary data was not received until today.

Our reports will be a week late because necessary data was not received until today.

<u>At this point in time</u>, we are not ready to make our final decision.

We are not ready to make our final decision.

Wordy expressions should also be edited to eliminate unnecessary words.

RELATED ASSIGNMENT:	EXERCISE 8.3, PAGE 123

■ ILLOGICAL INFORMATION

In some sentences, the words are clearly and concisely stated but are not logical. Consider this sentence as an example:

All our employees are not skilled in word processing.

The author does not really mean that *all* the employees are not skilled. The intended meaning is that *some* of the employees are not skilled. Ways to revise the sentence include:

Some of the employees are not skilled in word processing.

—or—

Not all our employees are skilled in word processing.

The word *not* was simply moved to the beginning to create a sentence that makes the proper sense.

Here is another example of a misplaced word:

Some elderly apartments are located on Bearry Street.

Actually, the apartments are not elderly; the term refers to the inhabitants. The sentence should be:

Some apartments for the elderly are located on Bearry Street.

The following are additional examples of illogical wording.

1. I would like to congratulate you on your promotion.

   Saying you *would like* to do something is not the same as doing it; the sentence suggests that you merely wish you could congratulate the person. An improvement would be

   Congratulations on your promotion.

2. The new computer is faster than any model on the market.

   The new computer cannot be faster than itself; it is only faster than other models. The sentence should be

   The new computer is faster than any other model on the market.

3. Try and answer the letter today.

   Only one activity is involved here so the word *and* is inappropriate. The wording should be

   Try to answer the letter today.

You must pay close attention to the content of the sentences you are reading to notice errors such as those contained in these examples.

RELATED ASSIGNMENT:	EXERCISE 8.4, PAGE 124

END-OF-CHAPTER ASSIGNMENT:	EXERCISES 8.5 THROUGH 8.10, PAGE 125 THROUGH 130

▤ EXERCISE 8.1

Complete the exercise below to practice proofreading for correctness of content. Edit the material to omit unnecessary information. Use revision marks to indicate changes that should be made. Use the space at the bottom of the page to rewrite or retype the paragraph. Be sure to proofread your final copy.

This letter is in response to your question about our next meeting. Our next meeting will be held in two weeks. The date of the meeting is March 21. The meeting will be held at 2 p.m. in the afternoon. The meeting will be held in the Fulton Building in the first floor conference room.

▤ EXERCISE

Complete the exercise below to practice proofreading for correctness of content. Edit the material to omit redundant information. Use revision marks to indicate changes that should be made. Use the space at the bottom of the page to rewrite or retype the paragraph. Be sure to proofread your final copy.

Thank you for asking for information about our weight reduction program for employees. Our program first began in 1960 when ten employees asked for help in becoming more healthy. We referred them back to our company physician, who told them they each needed to reduce their weight down by at least 20 pounds. We agreed to let the employees meet together at our plant facilities twice a week, every Tuesday and Thursday. We have been using exactly the same schedule ever since.

▤ EXERCISE

Complete the exercise below to practice proofreading for correctness of content. Edit the material to omit unnecessary information. Use revision marks to indicate changes that should be made. Use the space at the bottom of the page to rewrite or retype the paragraph. Be sure to proofread your final copy.

Please be advised that we have received your letter of recent date and have read its contents. Enclosed please find our catalog showing the products we have available at this point in time. We appreciate your interest in our company and would be interested in adding a new product. However, in view of the fact that our production capacity is at its limit, we cannot add any more products as of this time.

📄 EXERCISE 8.4

Complete the exercise below to practice your editing skill. Use revision marks to indicate changes needed. In the space below each sentence, rewrite or retype the sentence with appropriate wording. Be sure to proofread your final copy.

1. All of our employees are not taking refresher courses.

2. Our legal counsel has been appointed judge for the Criminal Court of Appeals.

3. One of our employees was feeling faint and asked for a cold glass of water.

4. All of the employees were asked to stay home, but all of them didn't; three came to work, anyway.

5. We do not make impersonal decisions using a computer; we do it on an individual basis.

▤ EXERCISE

Complete the exercise below to practice proofreading for correctness of content. Use revision marks to indicate changes that should be made. Use the space at the bottom of the page to rewrite or retype the paragraph. Be sure to proofread your final copy.

We have received your order. You did not give us enough information. Please tell us what shade of yellow drapes you prefer. The shades of yellow available are light, medium, and dark. We cannot ship your drapes until you send us this information.

▤ EXERCISE   8.6

Complete the exercise below to practice proofreading for correctness of content. Use revision marks to indicate changes that should be made. Use the space at the bottom of the page to rewrite or retype the paragraph. Be sure to proofread your final copy.

All our offices will not be closed for Memorial Day. Only the offices in Region 2 will be closed. In view of the fact that orders for our product are higher than anyone's, we will need to work on that day to keep up with demand. Please be advised that you will work your normal hours on that day. At this point in time, we plan to close some other day when production needs decrease.

📄 EXERCISE 8.7

Complete the exercise below to practice proofreading for correctness of content. Use revision marks to indicate changes that should be made. Rewrite or retype the material on another page. Be sure to proofread your final copy.

```
MEMORANDUM

TO:       All Employees

FROM:     Jorge Flanders, Plant Manager

DATE:     May 8, 19--

SUBJECT:  Election of Representatives

All employees are expected to meet together at 4 p.m. next week
on Friday afternoon, May 15, in the employees' lounge.  The
purpose of the meeting will be for the purpose of electing
employee representatives from each division.

Let me repeat again--the meeting will be Friday, May 15, at
4 p.m.

If you find that you cannot attend the meeting for any reason,
please be sure to tell your supervisor if you cannot be at the
meeting.

ds
```

▤ EXERCISE   8.8

Complete the exercise below to practice proofreading for correctness of content. Use revision marks to indicate changes that should be made. Rewrite or retype the material on another page. Be sure to proofread your final copy.

November 18, 19--

Mr. Angelo Browne
9752 Eastern
Tulsa, OK 74125

Dear Mr. Browne

We have received your letter of November 15 in which you asked for directions to our office nearest you. In reply to your letter, we wish to state that the closest office to you is located in the city of Bartlesville. It is located at 355 State Street.

Please be advised that the plant and office in Bartlesville will be closed next week for vacation.

Sincerely

Josephina Wellington
District Director

pk

▤ EXERCISE 8.9

Complete the exercise below to practice proofreading for correctness of content. Use revision marks to indicate changes that should be made. Rewrite or retype the information on another page. Be sure to proofread your final copy.

MEMORANDUM

TO: All Employees

FROM: Carey Denton, Director

DATE: August 15, 19--

SUBJECT: New Work Schedule

Please be advised that we will be reducing the number of workers next week in view of the fact that our sales have been low.

All of our employees will not be working next month. Instead, we will be using only half of the employees. The list of employees who will be working will be listed on the bulletin board at 4 p.m., Friday afternoon.

At this point in time, we do not know when the remaining employees will be asked to return back to their jobs.

lm

🗒 EXERCISE 8.10

Complete the exercise below to practice proofreading for correctness of content. Use revision marks to indicate changes that should be made. Rewrite or retype the information on another page. Be sure to proofread your final copy.

February 22, 19--

Mr. Fleming Fletcher
Dover Developers
100 Marquette
Tampa, FL 33601-2160

Dear Mr. Fletcher:

We have received your letter of February 12. In reply to your letter, we wish to state that we do not have the materials on hand at this time to repair your equipment. Although we do not have the material at this point in time, we do expect to receive a new supply of materials next Wednesday at 2 p.m. in the afternoon.

If you will be so kind as to bring your equipment to our shop at 2 p.m. on the afternoon of next Wednesday, we will be more than happy to repair it for you.

Please let us know each and every time you need our assistance.

Sincerely,

Billie Barnes
Customer Service

ek

Chapter

USE OF NUMBERS

What's Wrong Here?

Memo reminder: Your end-of-month report is due on February 30.

Numbers are used for a variety of purposes, and their accuracy is extremely important. The receiver of a message is more likely to correctly interpret a message with a misspelled *word* than one with an incorrect *number*. For example, the sentence below contains two errors.

Jerry and Alice spent $93.54 for office suplies.

The word *supplies* is obviously misspelled. The other error is in the dollar amount, which should have been $39.54! The reader would have no way of knowing that the amount was incorrect without additional information; a proofreader must be very careful in checking numbers.

Proofreading numbers requires checking for two types of errors:

1. errors involving numerical mistakes, such as transpositions, miscalculations, or inaccurate typing of number keys;

2. errors in style, in determining whether to express a number in figures or in words.

■ PROOFREADING FOR NUMERICAL ACCURACY

Methods of proofreading were studied and practiced in Chapter 1, with number combinations listed as one of the areas where proofreading errors often occur. Here is a quick review of some good proofreading techniques that are especially important in checking numbers:

1. Take your time; read slowly.

2. Read the material twice, once for typographical errors and once for content errors.

3. When accuracy is *extremely* important, such as in quantities and dollar amounts, use the cooperative method.

4. Verify the accuracy of all mathematical calculations.

An additional suggestion for proofreading numbers is to divide a figure of several digits into smaller parts. For example, to proofread *12,365,091*, you should read it in parts, such as 12—365—091. Even when no commas or decimals are included, checking just two digits at a time is a good proofreading technique. For example, *1825* would be read as 18—25.

RELATED ASSIGNMENT:	**EXERCISE 9.1,**	**PAGE 135**
	EXERCISE 9.2,	**PAGE 136**

■ PROOFREADING FOR CORRECTNESS OF NUMERICAL STYLE

Several generally accepted rules for expressing numbers are available to help you decide whether to express a number in figures or in words. A proofreader must know these rules (or consult a standard reference book) to be able to recognize accuracy of numerical style. The most commonly used rules for expression of numbers are listed and illustrated in this section.

Express the following items in *words:*

1. Numbers from one to ten, except when used in the same sentence with numbers above ten (be consistent). Watch for a few other exceptions to this rule in the items below.

    The enclosed procedures include five revisions.

    The meeting was attended by 15 regional managers.

    The new employees include 12 word processing operators and 2 supervisors.

2. Numbers used at the beginning of a sentence. Rewrite the sentence if the number is too long when expressed in words.

    Sixty-five members attended the association's annual meeting.

3. Approximate numbers.

    The remaining items will be sent to you in about thirty days.

4. Fractions, unless they are combined with whole numbers or are used for technical purposes. (Notice the spacing of the fraction in the second example.)

    We have remodeled two-thirds of our offices.

    Our employees received 2 ¾ hours of additional bonus pay last month.

5. The shorter number, when two related numbers are used together.

    I am enclosing twelve 15-page reports.

6. Names of streets numbered one through ten; houses and buildings with the number *one*.

    One North Main   1653 Tenth Avenue

7. Approximate ages, which are those that do not include month, day, and year.

Gregory was nineteen years old in January.

Freda's baby is 1 year, 2 months, and 10 days old.

8. Time of day except when followed by a.m. or p.m. or when giving both hours and minutes.

The board meeting will be held at three this afternoon.

All employees are expected to arrive by 8:30.

The building is locked each day at 5 p.m.

9. References to centuries or decades.

The Great Depression occurred in the early part of the twentieth century.

The data processing wing was added to the building in the sixties.

| RELATED ASSIGNMENT: | EXERCISE 9.3, PAGE 137 |
| | EXERCISE 9.4, PAGE 138 |

In addition to those instances described above when figures are to be used for numbers, express the following in *figures:*

1. Numbers in dates. Note that ordinals such as *st, rd,* and *th* are used with the numbers only when the day of the month precedes the name of the month.

The New Year's Eve party will be held on December 31 at the Paramount Inn.

The New Year's Eve party will be held on the 31st of December at the Paramount Inn.

2. Amounts of money and other decimal numbers. Zeros are omitted for whole dollar amounts when no other dollar and cent amounts are included in the sentence.

The registration fee for attending the conference is $25.

We spent 2.5 hours preparing the report.

Our records showed a difference in totals of 35 cents.

The bank balance was $435.00; our balance was $434.65.

Remember to carefully check the position of decimals. A figure of 2.75 incorrectly typed as 27.5 could cause significant problems if not corrected.

3. Numbers used after related words and abbreviations. The words preceding the numbers are often capitalized, but *page* and *paragraph* are not capitalized.

Please send Model 1645 shown on page 3 of your current catalog.

Item No. 475 of our last order was left out.

4. Numbers used with percentages and with units of weight and measure, such as inches, feet, ounces, pounds, and gallons. Use words, not symbols, for the units involved unless preparing statistical materials such as tables.

The office manager has ordered 5 dozen typewriter ribbons.

The aisle space allowed between desks is 3 feet 6 inches.

All employees will receive a pay increase of 8 percent.

5. Numbers used in addresses, other than lower-numbered addresses mentioned in the previous section.

Mr. Darryl Duncan
1257 North 35th Avenue
Minneapolis, MN 55415

Numbers in addresses must be checked carefully as any error would affect the efficient delivery of the mail. If the ZIP Code in the address above had been typed incorrectly as 45415, a document might be missent to a different area of the country.

The Postal Service encourages the use of ZIP + 4 in addresses to provide additional delivery directions. The four extra digits are separated from the ZIP Code by a hyphen.

Mr. Reginald Kovach
Carter Development
2135 Davis Avenue
Chicago, IL 60651-1506

Note: To create the plural form of a figure, add an *s;* no apostrophe is needed.

Several computer innovations occurred during the 1970s.

RELATED ASSIGNMENT:	EXERCISE 9.5, PAGE 139
	EXERCISE 9.6, PAGE 140

■ PROOFREADING FOR INCONSISTENT INFORMATION

Numbers and names should be checked with the original documents whenever possible. The proofreader should pay enough attention to the facts of a message to notice incorrect or inconsistent information. For example, one part of a message might be:

The three-day conference will be held in Nashville.

Another part of the message might include this sentence:

The dates of the conference are May 5 and 6.

As a proofreader, you should have noticed that only two dates were given, although it was referred to as a three-day conference. You would then have to determine the correct information.

Another item that should be checked is a date such as Friday, April 2. You should make sure that April 2 does fall on Friday. A third example is a reference to a page number. If a sentence refers to an illustration that is shown on page 3, you should check to be sure the correct page number has been used.

When information is presented in more than one place, you should be sure the information is the same each time. For example, if the text of a report refers to "a list of parts on page 10," you should check page 10 to be sure that the list is shown there. Dates and amounts, as well as names, are just a few of many other opportunities for error.

RELATED ASSIGNMENT:	EXERCISE 9.7, PAGE 141
	EXERCISE 9.8, PAGE 142

END-OF-CHAPTER ASSIGNMENT:	EXERCISE 9.9, PAGE 143
	EXERCISE 9.10, PAGE 144

📃 EXERCISE

Complete the exercise below to practice proofreading numbers. Compare the handwritten original copy with the typed copy. Use revision marks on the typed copy to indicate any errors.

1. *My meal expenses were: breakfast = $2.85, lunch = $4.20, supper = $7.10; total = $14.15*

   My meal expenses were: breakfast = $2.85, lunch = $4.20,

   supper = $7.10; total = $14.05.

2. *Please deliver this material to Everett Cooke at 100 Maine.*

   Please deliver this material to Everett Cooke at 1000 Maine.

3. *I will be out of the office on Friday, March 10, and Monday, March 31.*

   I will be out of the office on Friday, March 10, and Monday, March 31.

4. *The lowest price we have been able to get on airfare to New York is $588.*

   The lowest price we have been able to get on airfare to New York is $585.

5. *You will be receiving the original and four copies of the document.*

   You will be receiving the original and five copies of the document.

▤ EXERCISE

Complete the exercise below to practice proofreading numbers. Compare the handwritten original copy with the typed copy. Use revision marks to indicate errors on the typed copy.

MEMORANDUM

TO: Lynn Forrester, Purchasing
FROM: Terry Schuster, Engineering
DATE: April 5, 19--
SUBJECT: Materials Requested

The office supplies requisition we submitted to you on April 1 should have included a request for the following:

12 packages 4" x 6" index cards
Please add this item to our request.

MEMORANDUM

TO: Lynn Forrester, Purchasing

FROM: Terry Schuster, Engineering

DATE: April 5, 19--

SUBJECT: Materials Requested

The office supplies requisition we submitted to you on April 11 should have included a request for the following:

                21 packages   4" x 6" index cards

Please add this item to our request.

▤ EXERCISE

Complete the exercise below to practice proofreading numbers. Use revision marks to indicate corrections that should be made. Some sentences may be correct.

1. Please submit five copies of your proposed plan.

2. This year you will have ten holidays and 15 vacation days.

3. 14 new employees have been hired.

4. We expect to send about 40 of our plant employees to the conference.

5. Mr. Wurzton will spend about ½ of his time working on research.

6. Janet Gladstone missed 2 ½ days of work this week.

7. The plant will shut down for equipment repairs today at 4:30 p.m.

8. Our new offices are located at One 8th Avenue.

9. We are preparing our offices for the 21st century.

10. You will receive 65 personnel evaluations next week.

▤ EXERCISE 9.4

Complete the exercise below to practice proofreading numbers. Use revision marks to indicate corrections that should be made. Use the space at the bottom of the page to rewrite or retype the material.

The questionnaire was answered by 72 employees. Of this number, sixteen preferred the current method, ten wanted to change methods, and 46 had no opinion. I believe we will have to do some further research before a decision is made, as there was not a clear indication of a preference from the employees. If the 64 employees who had no opinion on the matter should decide for or against the change, our decision would be easier.

We should have at least twenty more who want the change than those who do not want the change before we consider adopting it.

▤ EXERCISE

Complete the exercise below to practice proofreading numbers, as well as the capitalization of related words. Use revision marks to indicate corrections that should be made. Some sentences may be correct.

1. Please reschedule the meeting of directors; the meeting will be held on Wednesday, June 15th.

2. A registration fee of $20.00 must be paid in advance.

3. The upgrading of the equipment will cost five hundred fifty dollars.

4. Your appointment with Mr. Davies has been changed from the 12th of August to the 1st of September.

5. Please refer to Page sixteen of the book for further information.

6. The cost of our raw materials has increased 10 percent in the past year.

7. We have substituted our latest version, Model 25, in place of the Model 24 you requested.

8. Thirty gallons of oil have been purchased for use by the maintenance department.

9. Please use No. 2 pencils for completing this form.

10. Paychecks will be received this month on the 29th.

▤ EXERCISE 9.6

Complete the exercise below to practice proofreading numbers. Use revision marks to indicate corrections that should be made. Use the space at the bottom of the page to rewrite or retype the paragraph. Be sure to proofread your final copy.

Our production report indicates that two thousand three hundred and twenty pounds of coal were used since the last reporting period ending February 1st. Our accounting records show an increase in costs of five cents per unit produced. However, our selling price per unit has increased; our selling price per unit is 40 cents higher than the total cost. Our production time per unit has decreased since we installed the new equipment. We can now produce each unit in 29.3 minutes. Total sales for this year so far are 14,250 units. Total sales for the same period last year were lower by thirty-seven units.

▤ EXERCISE   9.7

Complete the exercise below to practice proofreading numbers and related capitalization. Use revision marks to indicate corrections that should be made.

MEMORANDUM

TO: Managers and Supervisors

FROM: Jerry Latimer, General Manager

DATE: May 10th, 19--

SUBJECT: Communication Seminars

We have scheduled four seminars for managers and supervisors on the topic of oral communication. These seminars are designed to help you in working with employees in your departments.

Each manager and supervisor should plan to attend 1 of these seminars. The dates are June 10, June 21, July 6, and August 2nd. The seminars will be held in our main conference room. The conference room can hold fifteen persons for a meeting of this type, so we will need to schedule accordingly.

Please let me know by May 15th which of these three dates you would prefer.

fr

▤ EXERCISE

Complete the exercise below to practice proofreading numbers. Use revision marks to indicate corrections that should be made.

Please type an itinerary for Hank Ballentine.

Thurs., 6/5

3:15 p.m.	Leave Amarillo, National Flight #316
5:00 p.m.	Arrive Dallas; room reservation at Hotel Crowne
7:30 p.m.	Banquet, Hotel Crowne

Friday, 6/6

8:30 a.m.	Breakfast, Hotel Crowne
10:00 a.m.	Meeting, Convention Center
12:30 p.m.	Luncheon, Hotel Crowne
2:00 p.m.	Meeting, Convention Center
5:30 p.m.	Leave Dallas, National Flight #1211
7:00 p.m.	Arrive Amarillo

ITINERERY

Hank Ballentine

Thursday, June 5

3:15 p.m.	Leave Amarillo, National Flight No. 361
5:00 p.m.	Arrive Dallas; room reservation at Hotel Crowne
7:00 p.m.	Banquet, Hotel Crowne

Friday, June 6

8:30 a.m.	Breakfast, Hotel Crowne
10:30 a.m.	Meeting, Convention Center
12:30 p.m.	Luncheon, Hotel Crown
2:00 p.m.	Meeting, Convention Center
5:30 p.m.	Leave Dallas; National Flight No. 1211
7:00 p.m.	Arrive Amarillo

▤ EXERCISE

Complete the exercise below to practice proofreading numbers, including calculations. Use revision marks to indicate corrections that should be made.

Expense claim for Hank Ballentine's trip to Dallas:

6/5 airfare = $209; hotel = $58.80; banquet = $20; taxi = $15; regis. = $30

6/6 breakfast = $4.50; luncheon = $10; airfare = $209; taxi = $18; airport parking = $11

TRAVEL EXPENSE CLAIM

Date	Place Left	Place Arrived	Mileage	Airfare	Hotel	Bkfst.	Lunch	Dinner	Other	Total
6/5	Amarillo	Dallas		209.00	58.80			20.00	taxi— 15.00	302.80
									regis.— 30.00	30.00
6/6	Dallas	Amarillo		209.00		4.50	10.00		taxi— 18.00	214.50
									airport parking— 11.00	11.00
TOTALS				418.00	58.80	4.50	10.00	20.00	47.00	558.30

Name <u>Hank Ballentine</u>
Department <u>Sales</u>

Signature _____

Date _____

Advance	0.00
Balance	558.30

📄 EXERCISE

Complete the exercise below to practice proofreading numbers, abbreviations, and related capitalization. Use revision marks to indicate corrections that should be made.

Please type a purchase requisition for these items to be sent to my office by Nov. 31:

white correction fluid, 3/4 oz size (2 bottles)

1 box of staples, 1/4"

file folder labels, tan, 1/2" x 3/4", 1 box

1 box of No. 2 pencils

Cynthia Campbell—Personnel

PURCHASE REQUISITION

Requested by __Cynthia Campbell__   Date __November 10, 19—__

Deliver to __Personnel Department__   Date Needed __November 31, 19—__

Quantity	Description
2 bottles	¾-os. white correction fluid
1 box	¼' staples
1 box	file folder labels, tan, ½" × ¾"
1 box	No. 2 pencils

Chapter

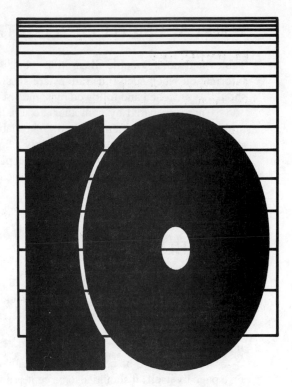

TABLES AND CHARTS

? What's Wrong Here?

VACATION PREFERENCES

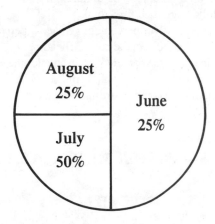

Tables and other graphic illustrations are often included in reports. Increased use is also being made of this type of illustration in letters and memos as a method of emphasis or as a way to make the message clearer.

Display materials such as tables and charts should be proofread, and they should be checked for accuracy and format.

Material shown in tables and charts is usually developed further in paragraph form or in a caption, so a comparison should be made to be sure that the information presented in word form is consistent with the information shown in the illustration. If there is a discrepancy and you cannot tell which information is correct, consult the author of the material. ■

■ PLACEMENT OF ILLUSTRATIONS

Tables and other graphic illustrations should be placed on the same page as the related text information when such illustrations are smaller than a full page. If possible, the table or chart should be preceded and followed by some discussion of the related information.

Charts prepared by computer are usually printed on a different page because a separate printing operation is often required. When tables and charts are shown on a separate page, they should be placed on the page immediately following the beginning of the discussion of the related topic. For example, if the discussion is four pages long, the illustration would be placed after the first page of the discussion. Only very detailed illustrations should be placed at the end of a letter or report.

■ TABLES

Tables are used to show specific numerical data. Any figures used must be checked for accuracy. In addition, mathematical calculations should be checked. Remember that some types of calculations do not use the decimal or base-10 system. For example, on a word processing productivity chart in which time spent on tasks must be calculated, you would change minutes to hours in intervals of *60*.

Tables should be centered horizontally across the page. If a table is large and is presented on a page by itself, it should also be centered vertically.

The title of the table should be centered and typed in all capital letters. If a subtitle is used, it should be centered a double space below the main title, using capital and lowercase letters. Two blank lines should separate the title section from the remainder of the table.

If the table has column headings, these headings should be centered over their columns and underscored; each column heading should be followed by one blank line.

The material within the columns can be single-spaced, double-spaced, or arranged in groups.

When a column of figures involves dollar amounts, place a dollar sign to the left of the first amount and to the left of the total (if any). The dollar sign at the top of the column should be aligned vertically with any dollar sign used for a total.

When a column of figures involves percentages, place a percent sign to the right of each figure unless the word *percent* is included in the column heading.

Although it is acceptable to use the percent sign in a table, the word *percent* should be used when discussing such materials in paragraph form. ■

The following table illustrates a common format for tables, as well as correct tabular use of dollar and percent signs.

SALES VOLUME BY PRODUCT

February, 19--

Product	Volume	Proportion of Total Volume
Mainframes	$1,050,000	46%
Microcomputers	375,000	16%
Terminals	150,000	7%
Printers	134,000	6%
Software	565,000	25%
Total	$2,274,000	100%

If you are checking worksheet or spreadsheet information on a computer, you will probably find it easier to print a copy of the information for proofreading purposes because many spreadsheets are too large to be seen on a screen at one time. Inconsistencies and other errors are difficult to detect when you cannot see the complete worksheet.

| RELATED ASSIGNMENT: | EXERCISE 10.1, page 149 |
| | EXERCISE 10.2, page 150 |

■ CHARTS

Charts are very effective for presenting information in picture form. The two most widely used styles are pie or circle charts and vertical bar charts. Charts should be proofread for accuracy of information and to ensure that the proportions shown are correct; otherwise, the picture may be distorted.

Pie Charts

Pie charts are used to show the proportion of parts to a whole item. Percentages or parts of a dollar are often used. For example, a pie chart could be used to show how a company allocates funds to the individual departments within the firm. The amounts would be expressed as percentages, and the total of all the percentages should equal 100 percent. An example of such a pie chart is shown below.

BUDGET ALLOCATIONS

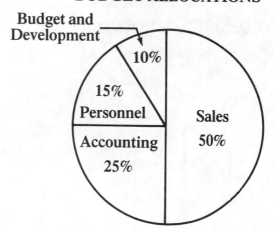

Some additional suggestions for good pie chart construction are

1. Label each segment with its identifying name and size; the name can be placed within its segment or outside, depending on the space available.

2. Each segment should be proportionately correct. For example, a segment representing 50 percent should be shown as half of the circle.

3. To make the illustration easier to read, present the segments in order from largest to smallest, starting at the top of the circle and going clockwise. However, if an *Other* or *Miscellaneous* section is included, that section should be shown last, regardless of size.

| RELATED ASSIGNMENT: | EXERCISE 10.3, page 151 |
| | EXERCISE 10.4, page 152 |

147

Bar Charts

Bar charts are used to compare quantities. The bars can run vertically or horizontally on the page. Many varieties of bar charts exist, but vertical bar charts are easy to construct and are the most widely used.

Some important guides for good bar chart construction are

1. The height of the bar indicates its quantity; the height of the bar should be proportionately accurate.

2. The quantity amounts should be labeled on the left side of the chart; the amounts should begin at zero at the bottom and increase in equal, evenly spaced amounts to the top.

3. Widths of individual bars should be the same; only the heights of the bars should vary.

4. If spacing is used between bars, the amount of space between bars should be equal.

5. If time periods are the basis for the bars, the bar for the earliest time should be shown on the left, with the time periods progressing in order to the right to the latest time period.

6. If no particular order exists, place the tallest bar on the left, proceeding to the right in order from tallest to smallest.

7. The bars should be clearly identified.

A vertical bar chart showing prices of a product at several stores is shown below. Compare this illustration with the guides above.

PRICES OF DESIRED UPHOLSTERY FABRIC

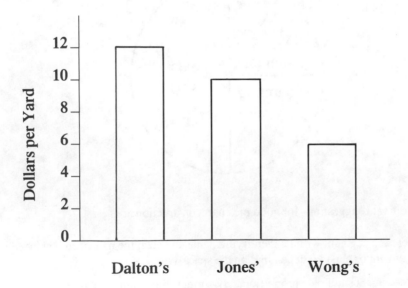

RELATED ASSIGNMENT:	EXERCISE 10.5, page 153 EXERCISE 10.6, page 154
END-OF-CHAPTER ASSIGNMENT:	EXERCISES 10.7 through 10.10, pages 155 through 158

▤ EXERCISE

Complete the exercise below to practice proofreading tables. Check the table format and the accuracy of the calculations. Use revision marks to indicate corrections.

January Sales Volume by Location

City	No. of Sales	Percent of Sales
Atlanta	885	15
Boston	782	13
Cincinnati	548	9
Denver	921	16
Los Angeles	1,516	21
New York	1,235	26
Total	4,887	100

☰ EXERCISE

Complete the exercise below to practice proofreading tables. Check the table format and the accuracy of the calculations. Use revision marks to indicate corrections.

NUMBER OF EMPLOYEES PER PLANT

Texas Locations

City	No. of Employees	Percent of Total
Abilene	305	22
Borger	210	15
Denton	150	15
Paris	190	14
Tyler	315	23
Waco	205	15
Total	1385	100

📋 EXERCISE

Complete the exercise below to practice proofreading charts. Check the chart format and the accuracy of the information. Use revision marks to indicate corrections. This chart is based on the information in Exercise 10.1.

JANUARY SALES VOLUME BY LOCATION

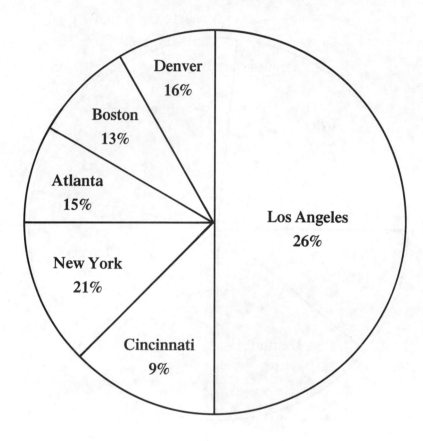

▤ EXERCISE   10.4

Complete the exercise below to practice proofreading charts. Use revision marks to indicate corrections. This chart is based on the information in the table in Exercise 10.2.

NUMBER OF EMPLOYEES PER PLANT
Texas Locations

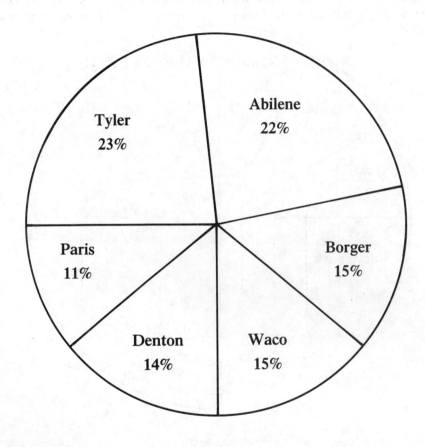

■ **EXERCISE**

Complete the exercise below to practice proofreading charts. Check the chart format and the accuracy of the information. Assume that the number of units shown in the chart is correct for each product type. Use revision marks to indicate corrections.

As shown in the chart below, we sold four types of products in March. We sold more units of candy than any other product and fewer units of cheese than any other product.

MARCH PRODUCT SALES IN UNITS

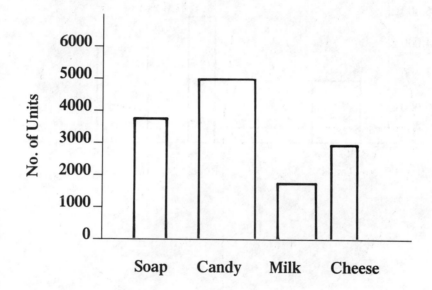

▤ EXERCISE

Complete the exercise below to practice proofreading charts. Check the chart format and the accuracy of the information. Assume that the number of units shown in the chart is correct for each product type. Use revision marks to indicate corrections.

We made a comparison of the cost of three brands of equipment. As shown in the chart below, the Rogers equipment is approximately $4,000 less expensive than the Tanns equipment.

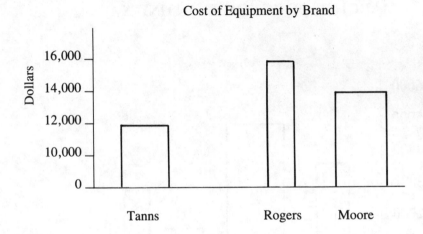

☰ EXERCISE

Complete the exercise below to practice proofreading tables. Check the table format and the accuracy of the calculations. Use revision marks to indicate corrections.

JANUARY TRAVEL EXPENSES

Dept.	Amount
Accounting	$ 59.00
Engineering	584.00
Legal	1,001.82
Personnel	2,371.25
Production	305.70
Sales	5,429.08
Total	$ 9750.85

▤ EXERCISE 10.8

Complete the exercise below to practice proofreading tables. Check the table format and the accuracy of the calculations. Use revision marks to indicate corrections needed. The amounts due are based on a charge of 20 cents per line produced.

WORD PROCESSING PRODUCTION

Charges for Week of June 5, 19--

| Department | Time Spent | | No. of Lines | Amount Due |
	Hours	Minutes	Produced	
Accounting	6	25	512	$ 120.40
Advertising	11	50	1,021	204.20
Engineering	26	15	2,215	434.00
Production	3	40	158	31.60
Purchasing	2	10	91	18.20
Sales	30	45	2,907	581.40
TOTALS	79	85	6.904	$1,389.80

▤ EXERCISE

Complete the exercise below to practice proofreading tables. Check the format of the table; assume that the dollar amounts are correct. Use revision marks to indicate corrections.

POTENTIAL PLANT LOCATIONS

Cost of Land

Location	Dollar Cost of Land
Nashville	210,000
Paducah	190,000
Clarksville	170,000
Jonesboro	150,000

▤ EXERCISE   10.10

Complete the exercise below to practice proofreading charts. Use revision marks to indicate corrections. This chart is based on the information in the table in Exercise 10.9.

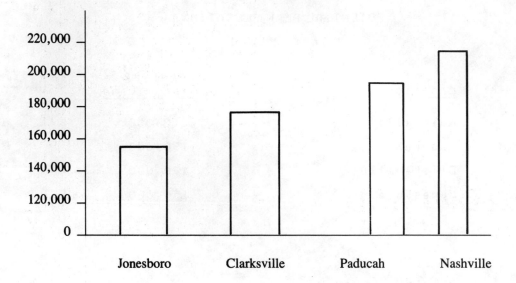

Chapter

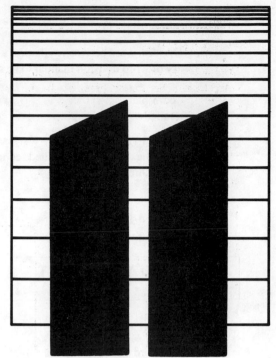

WORD DIVISION

?

What's Wrong Here?

Seen in a news article: Members were asked to re-
ad the budgets.

Words are divided at the end of the typing line to keep the right margin fairly even. In the past, there were many rules on how to divide words. Some rules are still closely followed, while others have been relaxed, partly due to technology.

Equipment is available today to make the task of word division easier. Some typewriters, word processors, and microcomputers automatically justify the right margin, leaving variable spacing within the line. The right margin is even, often without dividing words. One problem with this feature is that the number of blank spaces between words is sometimes distracting.

Another feature available on some equipment today is a *wraparound* feature that automatically moves to the next line any word that will not fit on the line being typed; the word is not divided. Although this feature eliminates word division, it sometimes creates widely varying and unattractive line lengths. The typist may choose to insert hyphens manually in such cases.

Improper word division may slow down or confuse the reader. The word must be divided where there is enough of the word to keep the reader moving at a normal pace. Care must be taken to be sure the reader will not have to stop and reread the material to understand the word.

 Since word division tends to make reading more difficult, words should be divided only when necessary to provide a reasonably attractive page. Many reference books suggest that no more than two consecutive lines end with hyphens and that no more than three lines on a page end with hyphens. ■

A good proofreader must be knowledgeable enough to recognize correct word division.

Here are the most widely used rules for word division:

1. Divide a word between syllables; a one-syllable word is not divided. Consult a dictionary or word division manual to be sure of the correct breaks in words.

   com-pare   (divided between two syllables)
   called   (not divided; one syllable)

2. When dividing a word, leave at least two letters on the first line and at least three letters on the next line. Each divided section of the word needs enough letters to avoid causing any reading difficulty.

   about   (not divided; first syllable has only one letter)
   admit-tedly   (not admitted-ly)
   ad-mittedly

RELATED ASSIGNMENT: EXERCISE 11.1,   PAGE 163
                           EXERCISE 11.2,   PAGE 164

3. If a word already contains a hyphen, divide at the hyphen.

   self-sufficient   (not self-suf-ficient)

4. Divide after a prefix or before a suffix unless the prefix or suffix has only one or two letters.

   delect-able   (not delecta-ble)
   non-existent   (not nonexis-tent)

RELATED ASSIGNMENT: EXERCISE 11.3,   PAGE 165
                           EXERCISE 11.4,   PAGE 166

5. Divide between double letters of a word unless the double letter is part of the ending of the root word itself.

   fol-low   fall-ing   ship-ping

6. Divide between two consecutive single-letter syllables.

   reconcili-ation

   continu-ation

RELATED ASSIGNMENT: EXERCISE 11.5,   PAGE 167
                           EXERCISE 11.6,   PAGE 168

7. Divide a compound word between the combined elements.

   how-ever

   under-estimated

8. Avoid dividing names, addresses, and dates. If one of these must be divided, divide at the point which will be easiest to read.

    Divide dates after month and day.

    November 22, / 1985   *not* November / 22, 1985

    Divide names before last name.

    Dr. Janice / Harmon   *not* Dr. / Janice Harmon

    Divide addresses between city and state.

    Albuquerque, / New Mexico

| RELATED ASSIGNMENT: | EXERCISE 11.7, PAGE 169 |
| | EXERCISE 11.8, PAGE 170 |

9. The last word on a page or the last word of a paragraph should not be divided. Also avoid dividing several consecutive lines on a page.

10. Avoid dividing words at places that would cause the reader to mispronounce the first part of the word and thus be slowed down in understanding the message.

    If *comedian* were divided this way:
                come-
                dian

    the reader would pronounce the first part as one syllable because it looks like the word *come*. The reader would be forced to reread the sentence to determine the correct word.

| END-OF-CHAPTER ASSIGNMENT: | EXERCISE 11.9, PAGE 171 |
| | EXERCISE 11.10, PAGE 172 |

▤ EXERCISE   11.1

Complete the exercise below to review word division. If the hyphen inserted in the word is placed in an acceptable location for word division, write a C in the column on the right. If the hyphen is not placed in an acceptable location for word division, rewrite the word in the column on the right and insert a hyphen in an acceptable location for word division. Some words may not contain an acceptable word division location. In that case, rewrite the word with no hyphen included.

1.	ni-ght	1.	_____
2.	on-ly	2.	_____
3.	com-fort	3.	_____
4.	a-gree	4.	_____
5.	mix-ed	5.	_____
6.	stand-ard	6.	_____
7.	cer-tain	7.	_____
8.	form-at	8.	_____
9.	ci-ty	9.	_____
10.	which-ever	10.	_____
11.	con-tain	11.	_____
12.	marg-in	12.	_____
13.	num-ber	13.	_____
14.	ex-cept	14.	_____
15.	dir-ect	15.	_____
16.	trai-ning	16.	_____
17.	ty-ped	17.	_____
18.	se-lect	18.	_____
19.	ro-tate	19.	_____
20.	spac-es	20.	_____

▤ EXERCISE

Complete the exercise below to practice proofreading word division. Use revision marks to indicate any changes needed.

```
                    Please add this sec-
                    tion to our office manual.
                    When typing letters, pla-
                    ce the salutation a dou-
                    ble space below the last
                    line of the inside ad-
                    dress or the attention
                    line.  Omit the saluta-
                    tion in the simplified let-
                    ter style.  Begin the sa-
                    lutation at the left marg-
                    in.  Use a colon after the
                    salutation if mixed punct-
                    uation is used; use no
                    punctuation mark if o-
                    pen punctuation is used.
```

▤ EXERCISE

Complete the exercise below to review word division. On the line to the right of each word, rewrite or retype the word and insert a hyphen in a location that would be appropriate for word division if the word should appear at the end of a line. If the word should not be divided, rewrite the word as shown.

1.	preconceived	1.	_____
2.	judging	2.	_____
3.	accountable	3.	_____
4.	friendliness	4.	_____
5.	self-contained	5.	_____
6.	happening	6.	_____
7.	last-minute	7.	_____
8.	percent	8.	_____
9.	fully	9.	_____
10.	favorably	10.	_____
11.	ex-president	11.	_____
12.	undo	12.	_____
13.	up-to-date	13.	_____
14.	readily	14.	_____
15.	unhappy	15.	_____
16.	childless	16.	_____
17.	ounce	17.	_____
18.	toward	18.	_____
19.	workable	19.	_____
20.	prefer	20.	_____

🗏 EXERCISE

Complete the exercise below to practice proofreading word division. Use revision marks to indicate locations where corrections should be made.

HOW TO TYPE MINUTES

Minutes are used to pro-
vide a written record of significant discussions and decisions
during a meeting. The minutes
should contain the date and time of
the meeting, as well as the time
the meeting was adjourned. Also included should be the names of
those persons who attended. Any
announcements are listed after th-
e disposition of the previous minutes.

The exact wording of motions
must be given in the minutes. Indicate whether the motion passed, failed, or was tabled.

📋 EXERCISE

Complete the exercise below to review word division. On the line to the right of each word, rewrite or retype the word and insert a hyphen in a location that would be appropriate for word division if the word should appear at the end of a line. If the word should not be divided, rewrite the word as shown.

1. graduation   1. _____

2. message   2. _____

3. yelled   3. _____

4. noontime   4. _____

5. mediation   5. _____

6. offshore   6. _____

7. selling   7. _____

8. latter   8. _____

9. mediocre   9. _____

10. shipped   10. _____

11. telltale   11. _____

12. worried   12. _____

13. accept   13. _____

14. manner   14. _____

15. common   15. _____

16. interrogate   16. _____

17. appreciation 17. _____

18. misspell   18. _____

19. messy   19. _____

20. challenge   20. _____

🖹 EXERCISE   11.6

Complete the exercise below to practice proofreading word division. Use revision marks to indicate corrections that should be made.

When you are addres-
sing envelopes, the mail-
ing address should be
single-spaced.   The
last line of the add-
ress should contain
the city, state, and
zip code.   If the en-
velope is used to
mail correspondence,
type the address exact-
ly as it appears in th-
e inside address.   On
a business envelope,
the address should be
typed about 12 lines
from the top and a-
bout 4 inches from the
left edge.

▤ EXERCISE

Complete the exercise below to improve your word division skill. Indicate with a hyphen an acceptable location to divide each item as if you were at the end of a typing line and needed to divide the item. If a hyphen would not be inserted but the material could be divided at the end of a line, indicate in the right margin the appropriate division location. If the item should not be divided, leave it as shown. Use revision marks to show the location of any inserted hyphen.

Mr. Alfonso Wolfe

May 13, 1985

2125 Aspen Avenue

afterthought

open-ended

doorway

cannot

Astrid Barlow

far-reaching

Farmington, New Mexico

blueprint

September 1, 1986

everything

Oklahoma City, Oklahoma

dateline

checkup

breakdown

backlog

Schenectady, New York

Ms. Melanie T. Chambers

☰ EXERCISE

Complete the exercise below to improve your proofreading of word division. Use revision marks to indicate corrections that should be made.

Please call Mr. Fred
K. Lundquist and ask
him the preferred loc-
ation of the doorstops
in the new building.
Mr. Lundquist and Mr.
Lorenzo Waters are un-
dertaking the task of
this renovation as an
extra job.   Normally,
they work in our Potta-
watomie County, Okla-
homa, area.   You will
also need to begin to
prepare the paychecks
for Mr. Lundquist and Mr.
Waters.   Their checks
should be sent to them
in Shawnee, Oklahoma.
Mail the checks on Nov-
ember 1, 19--.

▤ EXERCISE   11.9

Complete the exercise below to practice proofreading word division. Use revision marks to indicate corrections that should be made.

MEMORANDUM

TO: Secretarial Staff

FROM: Johnnetta Jabbour, Office Manager

DATE: September 29, 19--

SUBJECT: Filing Practices

Please follow these guidelines for filing so practices in all departments will be uniform:

1. File all correspondence in reverse chronologic-
    al order. This means that the most recent item
    of information will then be on top in each fold-
    er.

2. Use out *folders* rather than out cards when a who-
    le folder is removed from the file. This will
    provide a place to put materials that arrive dur-
    ing the time the folder is out of the file.

3. When you are typing a two-page letter, use both
    sides of the paper for the file copy to re-
    duce the number of pages being filed.

gl

▤ EXERCISE   11.10

Complete the exercise below to practice proofreading word division. Use revision marks to indicate corrections that should be made.

PLACING OUTGOING CALLS

Follow these procedures when placing outgoing calls:

1. Place the call at a time when the
   person you are calling is most likely to be there.

2. If you need information, plan your
   questions ahead of time.

3. Ask for directory assistance only if you cannot find the number yourself; then make a note of the number.

4. Dial carefully the number of the person to be called.

5. Let the telephone ring about ten times before you hang up.

6. Identify yourself when the other person answers.

Chapter

FORMAT

What's Wrong Here?

Short business letter:
    Dear George;
        No, thank you.
    Sincerely:
        Martin

Format refers to the arrangement of material on a page. Proper arrangement of letters, memos, and reports gives the reader a good impression of you and your firm. Many format rules are designed to help make the information easier to read and to give the page an attractive appearance.

■ LETTER FORMAT

Several letter formats are considered acceptable. The most widely used styles are shown in this chapter. As a proofreader, your main concerns about format are that an acceptable style is used and that the arrangement selected is used consistently throughout the letter. If you work for an organization that has a customary format, your job as a proofreader will be to ensure that the firm's preferences have been followed. You must be sure that all necessary letter parts are included, that the spacing is correct, and that the material is well balanced on the page.

The parts of a letter are listed below in the order they should appear in a letter. Some of these parts are optional.

1. date line (preceded by writer's address if no letterhead is used)

2. inside address

3. attention line (optional; use of colon after the word *Attention* is optional)

4. salutation (not used with the Administrative Management Society style)

5. subject line (optional except in AMS Style)

6. message

7. complimentary closing (not used in AMS style)

8. company name (optional)

9. author's name and title

10. reference initials

11. enclosure or attachment notation (used when appropriate)

12. copy notation (used when appropriate)

13. postscript (optional)

The two most commonly used letter styles are called the *block* style and the *modified block* style. In the block style, all letter parts start at the left margin. In the modified block style, some letter parts start at the center—the date line, the complimentary closing, and the writer's name and title. In the modified block style, the subject line can be placed either at the left margin or at the center of the typing line. In addition, paragraphs can be indented rather than blocked. However, indented paragraphs waste space and are not widely used for single-spaced materials. Two formats are shown on the next page. The parts of the letter have been identified for you by using the number of the letter parts given in the list above.

Guidelines exist for the amount of spacing between letter parts, but some variation is allowed depending on space limitations. The number of spaces between some parts should change when necessary to give the letter a balanced appearance. The following guides should be used:

1. The date line should be about 2 inches from the top of the page or at least a double space below the letterhead.

2. The inside address should be preceded by at least three blank lines. Additional blank lines can be used between the date and inside address if needed to spread the letter out over the whole page.

3. The attention line and salutation are each preceded and followed by one blank line.

4. The subject line is preceded and followed by one blank line unless using the AMS style described later in this chapter. When using the AMS style, the subject line is preceded and followed by two blank lines.

5. Individual paragraphs within the letter are single-spaced and are preceded and followed by one blank line.

6. The complimentary closing is preceded by one blank line; it is followed by one blank line if the company name is used and by at least three blank lines if the company name is not used. The company name is typed in all capital letters.

7. The author's name and title can be typed on one line or separated onto two lines, single-spaced. When the name and title are typed on one line, they should be separated by a comma. At least three blank lines should precede the line containing the author's name to allow ample space for the signature. Additional blank lines can be used above the author's name and title to spread the material out over the page.

8. The reference initials, enclosure or attachment notation, and copy notation should each be preceded and followed by a blank line. However, if space is limited, these blank lines can be omitted.

9. The postscript should be preceded by one blank line.

Notice that the paragraphs in the following examples have not been indented.

Ⓘ Date

Ⓞ
Name
Company
Street Address
City, State, Zip Code

Ⓞ Attention line

Ⓞ Salutation

Ⓞ Subject line

All letter parts begin at the left margin in the block style.

Ⓞ Individual parts of the letter are single-spaced with at least one blank line separating all major parts. In addition, each paragraph in the message section is separated by a blank line.

Ⓞ Complimentary closing

Ⓞ COMPANY NAME

Ⓞ Author's name
Author's title

Ⓞ Reference initials

Ⓞ Enclosure notation

Ⓞ Copy notation

Ⓞ Postscript

(Block Style)

Ⓘ Date

Ⓞ
Name
Company
Street Address
City, State, Zip Code

Ⓞ Attention line

Ⓞ Salutation

Ⓞ Subject line

In the modified block style letter, the date line and the closing lines start at the horizontal center of the page. All other letter parts begin at the left margin.

Ⓞ Individual parts of the letter are single-spaced with at least one blank line separating all major parts. In addition, each paragraph in the message section is separated by a blank line.

Ⓞ Complimentary closing

Ⓞ COMPANY NAME

Ⓞ Author's name
Author's title

Ⓞ Reference initials

Ⓞ Enclosure notation

Ⓞ Copy notation

Ⓞ Postscript

(Modified Block Style)

The trend is away from the use of indented paragraphs when the material is single-spaced. The purpose of the paragraph indention is to identify the beginning of a paragraph. When the paragraphs are single-spaced, a blank line is placed between each paragraph, which eliminates the need for the paragraph indention. ■

Another acceptable format is the AMS simplified style. In this style, the salutation and complimentary close are omitted. A subject line, typed in all capital letters, is used and is placed a triple space below the inside address and a triple space above the first paragraph of the letter. The name and the title of the author, typed in all capital letters, are placed at least four lines below the last paragraph of the letter. This letter style has become more popular in recent years because of the difficulty of determining appropriate salutations that give equal treatment to both sexes. With no salutation, this problem no longer exists. Until recent years, the salutation used in a letter addressed to an entire company was *Gentlemen*. Today, *Ladies and Gentlemen* is often used instead; or a letter style is used that requires no salutation.

The AMS style is shown below with the parts of the letter identified by using the numbers of the letter parts listed on page 173.

① Date

② Name
Company
Street Address
City, State, ZIP

⑤ SUBJECT LINE

⑥ In the AMS style letter, all letter parts begin at the left margin.

The salutation and complimentary close are omitted in this letter style. This style has increased in popularity in recent years.

⑨ AUTHOR'S NAME — TITLE
⑩ reference initials

(AMS Style)

RELATED ASSIGNMENT:	EXERCISES 12.1 THROUGH 12.3, PAGES 181 THROUGH 183

Another aspect of letter format to be checked is the punctuation style used with the salutation and complimentary closing. The most widely used styles are *mixed* and *open*. When using mixed punctuation, a colon is placed after the salutation with a comma placed after the complimentary close. When using open punctuation, no punctuation follows either the salutation or the complimentary close. In other words, if a colon follows the salutation, a comma must follow the complimentary close. If no punctuation follows the salutation, no punctuation follows the complimentary close. These two punctuation styles are illustrated on the following page.

```
Date                                    Date

Name                                    Name
Company                                 Company
Street Address                          Street Address
City, State, ZIP                        City, State, ZIP

Salutation:                             Salutation

When mixed punctuation is               No punctuation is used after
used in business writing, a             the salutation, and no
colon is placed after the               punctuation is used after the
salutation and a comma is               complimentary close when the
placed after the compli-                open punctuation style is used.
mentary close. Standard                 Standard punctuation is used
punctuation is used for the             for the message.
message.
                                        Complimentary close
Complimentary close,
                                        Author's name
Author's name
                                        reference initials
reference initials
```

(Mixed Punctuation)   (Open Punctuation)

These two punctuation styles are appropriate for use with either the block style or the modified block style of letter.

RELATED ASSIGNMENT: EXERCISE 12.4,   PAGE 184

If a letter is more than one page long, you must check the format of the heading for the second and succeeding pages. The second and any additional pages are typed on plain paper, with the heading about 1 inch below the top of the page. The heading contents should be checked with the first page to be sure the name and date are the same. In addition, you should be sure the pages are numbered consecutively.

Two acceptable formats are

Horizontal:

```
Mr. Juan Suarez              2           July 5, 19--
```

Vertical:

```
Mr. Juan Suarez
Page 2
July 5, 19--
```

The vertical arrangement is easier to type because each line starts at the left margin, but it does use more lines for the information. After either the horizontal or vertical heading, the typist should triple-space before continuing the message; therefore, two blank lines should appear between the heading and the message's first line.

■ MEMORANDUM FORMAT

A memorandum is an informal format for sending a written message. A letter format is used for written messages going outside the firm, and a memorandum format is often used for messages to other employees within the firm.

Most business firms have a printed memorandum form. In addition to the company name, the stationery usually contains four printed headings, *to, from, date,* and *subject.* The arrangement of these headings varies considerably. The most common arrangement has all four headings printed on the left. When a printed form is used, the left margin is usually set two spaces to the right of the longest heading.

When the memorandum title and headings must be individually typed, the headings should be aligned on the left for ease of typing. They are usually typed in all capital letters. The title, *Memorandum,* can be centered or placed at the left margin, preferably in all capitals, 1 ½ inches from the top of the page.

Some additional format guides for memorandum typing are

1. Side and bottom margins of at least 1 inch should be used.

2. The information beside each heading should be aligned two spaces to the right of the longest heading.

3. Two blank lines should be placed between the last line of the heading section and the beginning of the message.

4. No signature line is used. Most writers initial or sign beside their names in the heading section.

5. Reference initials should be placed in lowercase letters a double space below the last line of the message.

Two illustrations of memorandum format follow. The first illustration shows the appearance when the title and headings are individually typed; the second illustration shows the appearance when a printed form is used.

```
                        MEMORANDUM

    TO:        Reader's Name

    FROM:      Author's Name

    DATE:      Current Date

    SUBJECT:   Major Topic

    A memorandum is used for informal written messages within a
    business.

    The message begins a triple space below the last line of the heading.
    The message is single-spaced, with a blank line separating each
    paragraph.   No signature line is used at the end of the message.

    reference initials
```

```
Memorandum

  TO:        Reader's Name


  FROM:      Author's Name


  DATE:      Current Date


  SUBJECT:   Major Topic

             A memorandum form may be used.  A memorandum
             form provides the headings at the top of the page, usually
             all on the left side.  Some variation exists in the order of
             presentation of the information at the top of the
             memorandum.

             When a form memorandum is used, it is more efficient
             to set the left margin at the location where the heading
             information is to be typed rather than at the left edge of
             the headings.  Using this method allows the entire
             memorandum to be typed without the need for any tab
             settings.

             reference initials
```

RELATED ASSIGNMENT: **EXERCISE 12.5,   PAGE 185**
                            EXERCISE 12.6,   PAGE 186

■ REPORT FORMAT

Reports are considered more formal presentations of information than either letters or memos. Many types of reports are prepared in businesses; most reports travel upward to higher levels of the organization.

Numerous style manuals are available for detailed instructions, and some firms develop their own manuals. Employees should follow company preferences in report format.

The guides listed in this chapter are commonly used and will give you a good background of the types of format errors to watch for. The most important aspect to check is consistency. The chosen style should be followed consistently throughout the report.

Margins

Margins should be at least 1 inch on all sides, with a top margin of 1 ½ inches to 2 inches on the first page.

Headings

The main heading, usually reserved for the title, is centered and typed in all capital letters. The remaining lower-level headings can be done in several styles as long as their relative importance is apparent and the chosen style remains consistent throughout the report. Headings in all capital letters are considered more important than those in a combination of capital and lower case.

Centered headings are considered more important than those on the left. Headings placed on a line by themselves are considered more important than those on the same line as the beginning of a paragraph. Most style manuals recommend underscored headings when they are not typed in all capital letters; they do *not* recommend the use of the underscore when the heading is in all capital letters. The heading format shown below is widely used.

```
                           MAIN HEADING

                          Centered Heading

  Side Heading

      Paragraph Heading
```

Spacing

Many reports are double-spaced, and paragraphs are indented. Some informal reports are single-spaced to reduce the number of pages. Special spacing rules apply to headings. In most cases, the main heading should be followed by two blank lines. However, if it is immediately followed by a subheading, only one blank line follows the main heading, and two blank lines follow the subheading. All headings within the report should be preceded by an extra blank line. When tables and other graphic illustrations are included within the text of a report, at least one extra blank line should be provided above and below these materials. Additional information related to tables and other graphic aids is given in Chapter 10.

Page Numbers

A page number is not required on the first page of a report. However, if a number is used for that page, it should be centered horizontally about ½ inch above the bottom of the page. Unless the report is to be bound at the top, succeeding pages are numbered in the upper right corner, even with the right margin. Some variation exists among style manuals as to how far down from the top the page number should be placed. One popular method recommends that the page number be typed on the fourth line from the top, followed by two blank lines before beginning the paragraphs. This method provides the required 1-inch top margin.

| RELATED ASSIGNMENT: | EXERCISE 12.7, PAGE 187 |
| | EXERCISE 12.8, PAGE 188 |

| END-OF-CHAPTER ASSIGNMENT: | EXERCISE 12.9, PAGE 189 |
| | EXERCISE 12.10, PAGE 190 |

▤ EXERCISE 12.1

Complete the exercise below to practice proofreading letter format. Use revision marks to indicate corrections that should be made.

February 6, 19--

Lambert Company
3582 Leffingwell
Hartford, CT 06141-1141

Attention David Lippert, Purchasing

Subject: Your Request for Credit Purchases

Ladies and Gentlemen

Thank you for your request for information concerning purchases of merchandise on credit. We do allow companies of your size to make purchases on credit if they meet our guidelines.

   In order for us to determine if your company meets our credit standards, please fill out and return the enclosed application form. As soon as we receive the information, we will have it evaluated by our credit analyst and will send you the results as soon as we have them.

Sincerely

Marcus Craighead
Credit Department

lf

Enclosure

▤ EXERCISE   12.2

Complete the exercise below to practice proofreading letter format. Use revision marks to indicate corrections that should be made. This is the same letter as the one in Exercise 12.1, except that a modified block style is used.

                                              February 6, 19--

Lambert Company
3582 Leffingwell
Hartford, CT 06141-1141

Attention David Lippert, Purchasing

Subject: Your Request for Credit Purchases

Thank you for your request for information concerning purchases of merchandise on credit. We do allow companies of your size to make purchases on credit if they meet our guidelines.

In order for us to determine if your company meets our credit standards, please fill out and return the enclosed application form. As soon as we receive the information, we will have it evaluated by our credit analyst and will send you the results as soon as we have them.

Sincerely

Marcus Craighead
Credit Department

lf

▤ EXERCISE   12.3

Complete the exercise below to practice proofreading letter format. Use revision marks to indicate corrections that should be made. This is the same letter as the one in Exercise 12.1, except that the AMS simplified letter style is used.

February 6, 19--

Mr. David Lippert, Purchasing
Lambert Company
3582 Leffingwell
Hartford, CT 06141-1141

YOUR REQUEST FOR CREDIT PURCHASES

Thank you for your request for information concerning purchases of merchandise on credit. We do allow companies of your size to make purchases on credit if they meet our guidelines.

In order for us to determine if your company meets our credit standards, please fill out and return the enclosed application form. As soon as we receive the information, we will have it evaluated by our credit analyst and will send you the results as soon as we have them.

                    MARCUS CRAIGHEAD - CREDIT DEPARTMENT

lf

Enclosure

▤ EXERCISE

Complete the exercise below to check your knowledge of punctuation styles. Use revision marks to indicate errors in punctuation styles. Some punctuation may be correct as shown.

Letter No. 1

Dear Mr. Sampson,

xxxxxxxxxxxxxxxxxxxxxxxxxxxxxxxxxxxxxxxxxxxxxxxxxxxxxxxxxxxxxxxxxxxxxxxxxxxxx
xxxxxxxxxxxxxxxxxxxxxxxxxxxxxxxxxxxxxxxxxxxxxx.

Sincerely yours,

Letter No. 2

Dear Dr. Friend:

xxxxxxxxxxxxxxxxxxxxxxxxxxxxxxxxxxxxxxxxxxxxxxxxxxxxxxxxxxxxxxxxxxxxxxxxxxxxx
xxxxxxxxxxxxxxxxxxxxxxxxxxxxxxxxxx.

Sincerely yours

Letter No. 3

Dear Mr. McCabe:

xxxxxxxxxxxxxxxxxxxxxxxxxxxxxxxxxxxxxxxxxxxxxxxxxxxxxxxxxxxxxxxxxxxxxxxxxxxxx
xxxxxxxxxxxxxxxxxx.

Sincerely yours,

Letter No. 4

Dear Ms. Jonas

xxxxxxxxxxxxxxxxxxxxxxxxxxxxxxxxxxxxxxxxxxxxxxxxxxxxxxxxxxxxxxxxxxxxxxxxxxxxx
xxxxxxxxxxx.

Sincerely yours

▤ EXERCISE   12.5

Complete the exercise below to practice proofreading memorandum format. Use revision marks to indicate corrections that should be made.

MEMORANDUM

TO: All Employees

FROM: Marcia Franke, Personnel Director

DATE: December 10, 19--

SUBJECT: New Contract for Plant Workers

   Our new contract for plant employees has been approved by
both management and the union. Changes for next year include
an 8 percent salary increase and bonus vacation days for
workers with perfect attendance records.

   The new contract goes into effect on January 1.
wr

■ EXERCISE   **12.6**

Complete the exercise below to practice proofreading memorandum format. Use revision marks
to indicate corrections that should be made.

MEMORANDUM

TO: All Employees

FROM: Sonny Kimball, Manager

DATE: March 2, 19--

SUBJECT: New Holiday

All employees will have an extra holiday this year.   Each employee will have
a birthday holiday!

The new holiday plan will take effect May 1.   To take advantage of your
birthday holiday, turn in your absence request at least one week in
advance of your birthday.

                         Sincerely,

                         Sonny, Kimball, Manager

kp

▤ EXERCISE   12.7

Complete the exercise below to practice proofreading report format. Use revision marks to indicate corrections that should be made. Assume that the material below is the first page of a report.

1

SHOULD THE WORD PROCESSING STAFF BE INCREASED?

Introduction

Purpose of the Study

The purpose of this report is to study the needs of this company related to its use of the word processing facilities. The result of this study should be a determination of the company's needs for personnel in the word processing center.

Methods of Obtaining Information

Information for this report was gathered by analyzing the quantity of work entering the word processing facility and the waiting time before each item is produced in final form. Additional information was obtained by surveying companies of similar type and size to determine the sizes of their word processing operations, including volume of work and number of staff employees.

Scope and Limitations

This report studies only the staff needs in the word processing center. No consideration is given to the staff needs of other offices or the effect on word processing if an increase were made in staff in other departments.

▤ EXERCISE   12.8

Complete the exercise below to practice proofreading report format. Use revision marks to indicate corrections that should be made. Assume that the material below is the last page of the report started in Exercise 12.7.

Conclusions and Recommendations

As shown in the previous section, the word processing center staff is unable to keep up with the quantity of material coming into that office. The questionnaire sent to similar companies indicated that our staff is considerably smaller than the staff of other firms with a volume of work about the size of ours.

Based on the information found, the following recommendations are made:

The number of employees in the word processing center should be increased by three.

A review of the efficiency of the word processing office should be made in six months to be sure that a significant increase in output has occurred by adding to the staff.

Additional annual reviews should be made of the quantity and quality of work produced in the word processing center.

4

▤ EXERCISE   12.9

Complete the exercise below to practice proofreading letter format. Use revision marks to indicate corrections that should be made. Assume that the material below is the first page of a two-page letter.

August 11, 19--

Ms. Aurelia Johnson
3249 Neighborly Way
Eugene, OR 97440

Subject: Your Account Balance

Dear Ms. Johnson:

Have you been enjoying your piano you purchased from us in May? You selected one of the finest pianos available today. It should be giving you many hours of pleasure.

As you may know, a payment on your account is overdue. Your account balance is $1,257.31; a payment of at least $125 should have been made last month.

Is there some problem with the piano? Of course, we would like to know if there is something wrong with the piano that perhaps we could fix. When we last heard from you, the piano was performing well; we would certainly be glad to check it if there are any problems that have arisen since that time.

If there is some other reason you have been unable to make a payment on your account, we might be able to be of some assistance there, too. Our credit department will be happy to work with you to arrange a different plan if you need one.

📃 EXERCISE   12.10

Complete the exercise below to practice proofreading letter format. Use revision marks to indicate corrections that should be made. Assume that the material below is the last page of the two-page letter started in Exercise 12.9.

Ms. Aurelia Johnson
August 11, 19--

We certainly want you to be able to continue to enjoy your piano. It is the type of investment that you will never regret.

Please call Carolina Carlson to set up an appointment to discuss your account. We will be happy to help you in any way we can.

Sincerely

Johnnie Begley, Credit Manager
PIANOS AND MORE

jt

IN-BASKET SIMULATION

■ JOB SETTING

You are a word processing center supervisor in the Phoenix regional office of a multinational manufacturing company. You are responsible for checking the items typed in the word processing center. Materials are typed from taped dictation, from handwritten notes, or from previously typed rough drafts.

The people in your company who regularly use the services of the word processing center are shown on the organization chart below.

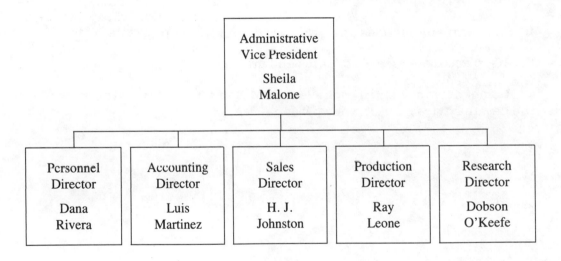

Today is Friday, September 2. The twenty items on the following pages have been typed by word processing employees and are on your desk waiting for your approval. Use revision marks to indicate changes that should be made. If an item is correctly typed, place your initials in the lower right corner of the document to indicate your approval. Here is this month's calendar:

SEPTEMBER

S	M	T	W	T	F	S
				1	2	3
4	5	6	7	8	9	10
11	12	13	14	15	16	17
18	19	20	21	22	23	24
25	26	27	28	29	30	

If you must tear out the following page, photocopy this page for later reference.

🗐 TASK 1

Proofread the memorandum below and edit as necessary. Use revision marks to indicate changes needed. This document was typed from the handwritten material shown on page 193.

MEMORANDUM

TO: All Employees

FROM   Dana Rivera, Personnel Director

DATE: September 2, 19--

SUBJECT   Company Vehicles

Use the following procedure in the future when using comapny vehicles:

1.   Be sure to make arrangements one full day in advance of the date you
     need the company vehicle.

2.   Use company vehicles only when traveling on company business.

3.   Keep accurate records of dates and mileage.

4.   Do not drive a company vehicle to your home, turn it in at the end of
the day and drive home in your personal vehicle.

rr

▤ TASK 1

Memo to all employees

Subject ⌐ Company Vehicles

Use the following ~~procedure~~ procedure in the future when using company vehicles:

1. Be sure to make arrangements one full day in advance of the date you need the company vehicle.

2. Use company vehicles only when traveling on company business.

3. Keep accurate records of dates and mileage.

4. Do not drive a company vehicle to your home, turn it in at the end of the day and drive home in your personal vehicle.

Dana Rivera

▤ TASK 2

Proofread the letter below and edit as necessary. Use revision marks to indicate changes needed. This document was typed from the rough draft shown on page 195. This letter should be in block style.

September 2, 19--

Mr. Kelly Kimp
McGill Products, Inc.
3342 Willow
Columbia, MO 65205-1260

Dear Mr. Kimp:

As you requested we have changed the date of delivery of your order form September 28 to September 21.

We checked with our delivery service in your area and found that it would be no problem to change the delivery date once we get the materials to them. We hope this gives you a clear picture of are service attitude.

Please let us know at your earliest convenience if we can help again in anyway.

                    Sincerely yours,

                    H. J. Johnson
                    Sales Director

pk

▤ TASK 2

September 2, 19--

Mr. Kelly Kimp
McGill Products, Inc.
3342 Willow
Columbia, MO 65205-1206

Dear Mr. ~~Kelly~~ Kimp:

As you requested we have changed the date of delivery of your order form
September 28 to September 21.

We checked with our delivery service in your area and found that it would
be no problem to change the delivery date once we get the materials to
them. We hope this gives you a clear picture of are service attitude.

Please let us know at your earliest convenience if we can help again in
anyway.

                          Sincerely yours,

                          J. H. Johnston
                          Sales Director

pk

🗐 TASK 3

Proofread the memo below and edit as necessary. Use revision marks to indicate changes needed. This document was typed from taped dictation.

MEMO

TO: All Employees

FROM: Dana Rivera, Personnel Director

DATE: September 2, 19--

SUBJECT: Master Keys

We have had a report that one employees' set of master keys has either been missed placed or stolen.   For security reasons, we are having the locks changed and new master keys made.   These keys will be ready Tuesday, September 6th.

Each employee will be issued a new set of master keys when he turns his current set of keys into Iris LeCrone in room 350.

lb

▤ TASK 4

Proofread the memo below and edit as necessary. Use revision marks to indicate changes needed. This document was typed from the handwritten material shown on page 199.

TO: Dobson O'Keefe, Research Director

FROM: Dana Rivera, Personnel Director

DATE: September 2, 19--

SUBJECT: Acapulco Trip

A slight chance has been made in your trip schedule for your International Research Conference in Acapulco. Your are not scheduled to Leave Phoenix at 8 a.m. on September 29 on International Airways Flight No. 358. Your arrival time in Acapulco will be 2:30 p.m.

Your complete itinerary will be sent to you as soon as it is completed in the work processing center.

pm

▤ **TASK 4**

Memo to D. O'Keefe
   about Acapulco trip

A slight change has been made in
your trip schedule for your
International Research Conference
in Acapulco. You are now
scheduled to leave Phoenix at
8 a.m. on September 29 on
International Airways Flight
no. 358. Your arrival time
in Acapulco will be 2:30 p.m.
A Your complete itinerary will
be send to you as soon as it
is completed in the word
processing center.

                        D. Rivera

📋 TASK 5

Proofread the minutes below and edit as necessary. Use revision marks to indicate changes needed. This document was typed from taped dictation.

MINUTES

Staff Meeting

August 31, 19--

The monthly staff meeting was held on Wednesday, August 30, at 2 p.m. in the afternoon in the conference room.   Those present included Dana Rivera, Luis Martinex, H. J. Johnston, Roy Leone, and Dobson O'Keefe. Sheila Malone presided at the meeting.

   The major item discussed was the implementation plan for the use of employee involvement groups.   Ray Leone reported that the test groups being used in his department had been somewhat successful, but needed some changes. He stated that Robert Reed did a better job of leading the meetings than anyone. His recommendation was that smaller groups be used and that each employee be encouraged to attend his assigned weekly meeting.

Additional discussion was held concerning methods of improving the group meetings.   The following recommendations were made:

1. Limit the size of each group to 8 members.

2. Conduct seminars for supervisors in methods of encouraging employee discussion.

3. Limit the meeting times to 30 minutes per week.

The next staff meeting will be held on Wednesday, September 28, at 2 p.n.

Luis Martinez, Secretary

jk

🗐 TASK 6

Proofread the itinerary below and edit as necessary. Use revision marks to indicate changes needed. This document was typed from the handwritten material shown on page 203.

ITINERARY—Dodson O'Keefe

Internation Research Conference

Acapulco, Mexico

September 29–31, 19--

Thursday, September 29

9 a.m.   Leave Phoenix.
                International Airways Flight No. 358.

3 p.m.   Arrive Acapolco.

                Hotel accomodations: Reservation at
                La Mansion de Las Americas (two nights).

Friday, September 30

10 a.m.   International Research Conference.
                El Presdiente Suite,
                La Mansion de Las Americas.

8 p.m.   Banquet.
                La Cabana,
                La Mansion de Las America.

Saturday, October 1

9 a.m.   Breakfast meeting.
                El Cafe del Sur
                La Mansion de Las Americas.

1 p.m.   Leave Acapulco.
                International Airways Flight no. 156.

5 p.m.   Arrive Phoenix.

▤ TASK 6

ITINERARY - Dobson O'Keefe
International Research Conference
Acapulco, Mexico
Sept. 29-31, 19--

<u>Thurs., Sept. 29</u>

9 a.m.   <u>Leave Phoenix.</u>
           International Airways
           Flight No. 358.

3 p.m.   <u>Arrive Acapulco.</u>

           <u>Hotel accomodations:</u>
           Reservation at La Mansion
           de Las Americas (two nights).

<u>Fri., Sept. 30</u>

10 a.m.   <u>International Research</u>
           <u>Conference.</u>
           El Presidente Suite,
           La Mansion de Las
           Americas.

8 p.m.   <u>Banquet.</u>
           La Cabana,
           La Mansion de Las
           americas.

<u>Sat., Oct. 1</u>

9 a.m.   <u>Breakfast meeting.</u>
           El Cafe del Sur,
           La Mansion de Las
           americas.

1 p.m.   <u>Leave Acapulco.</u>
           International Airways
           Flight No. 156.

5 p.m.   <u>Arrive Phoenix.</u>

▤ TASK 7

Proofread the letter report below and edit as necessary. Use revision marks to indicate changes needed. This document was typed from taped dictation.

September 2, 19--

TO OUR STOCKHOLDERS:

We are pleased to announce that we are declaring a divident of $2.25 per share as a result of our profits for the fiscal year just completed.

Shown below is a listing of the earnings per share for the past 3 years, which indicates that this years' amount is an increase over the past years.

EARNINGS PER SHARE (EPS)

198X–198Z

Date	ESP
September, 198X	$1.25
September, 198Y	1.75
September, 198Z	2.25

Although we have alot of stockholders, we always welcome questions from each and every person who is interested in our firm. Please refer back to our latest annual report for additional information on the details of our production and sales.

▤ TASK 8

Proofread the purchase requisition below and edit as necessary. Use revision marks to indicate changes needed. This document was typed from the handwritten material shown on page 207.

PURCHASE REQUISITION

	ACCOUNT NUMBER					AMOUNT
REQUESTED BY Dobson O'Keefe **DATE** 9-2- -	Fund	Function	Sub-Acct.	Object Code	N/R	
						18.60
APPROVED BY _____						
AUTHORIZATION FOR EQUIPMENT PURCHASES						

AUTHORIZED _____

SHIPMENTS TO BE ADDRESSED AS FOLLOWS

DEPARTMENT Research   **TEL. EXT.** 2442

APPROVED _____   **PURCHASING AGENT**

DELIVER TO _____ Main _____ 308
     BLDG   ROOM

INDICATE DATE REQUIRED _____

ATTENTION OF Dopson O'Kefe

STOCK NUMBER	PLEASE GIVE FULL DESCRIPTION AND COMPLETE SPECIFICATIONS ATTACH WRITTEN QUOTATIONS IF SUCH WERE RECEIVED	QUANTITY	UNIT PRICE	AMOUNT
	Scotch transparent tape, 3/4 in. x 108 ft.	10	1.08	10.80
	Bostitch staples, 1/4 in., 5,000/box	12	.65	7.80
	Total			28.60

📑 TASK 8

Please type a requisition for
the following items:

10 rolls Scotch Transparent tape,
    3/4" x 108' ($1.08 per roll)

12 boxes Bostitch staples,
    1/4", 5,000/box
        (65¢ per box)

D. O'Keefe

▤ TASK 9

Proofread the 2nd page of this letter and edit as necessary. Use revision marks to indicate changes needed. This document was typed from the rough draft shown on page 209. This letter should be in modified block style.

Dr. LeRoy LeBalnc
Page 2
September 2, 19--

We appreciate your patients in waiting on these products.   According to our latest estimate, these items should be completed by Friday, September 23 and will be delivered to you the following Monday.

In the meantime, please except the enclosed coupon for a 20 percent discount on our next purchase from us.

Sincerely yours,

H. J. Johnston
Sales Director

le

Enclosure

▤ TASK 9

Dr. LeRoy LeBlanc
September 2, 19--
Page 2

We appreciate your patients in waiting on these products. According to our latest estimate, these items should be completed by Friday, Sept. 23 and will be delivered to you the following Monday.

In the mean time, please ___ the enclosed coupon for a ~~twenty~~ 20 percent discount on our ___chase from us.

Sinc___ ___urs,

H. J. Johnston
Sales Director

le

Enclosure

▤ TASK 10

Proofread the memo below and edit as necessary. Use revision marks to indicate changes needed. This document was typed from taped dictation.

MEMO

TO: All Employees

FROM: Dana Rivera, Personnel Director

DATE: September 2, 19--

SUBJECT: Secretarial Position

A new secretarial position will be available next month. This position will be as executive secretary for Administrative Vice President Shiela Malone.

Any employee who is interested in applying for the position should contact my desk to schedule an appointment for an interview. Applicants must have a high school diploma and one-year of secretarial experience or equilivant training, as well as proficient secretarial skills.

Each and every employee who indicates an interest will be given an interview and a skills proficiency test. Appointments will start one week from today, Friday, September 10, 19--.

jf

▤ TASK 11

Proofread the memo below and edit as necessary. Use revision marks to indicate changes needed. This document was typed from the handwritten material shown on page 213.

MEMO

TO: Sheila Malone, Administrative Vice President

FROM: H. J. Johnston, Sales Director

DATE: September 2, 19--

SUBJECT: Quarterly Sales Meeting

I have just returned from attending the quarterly sales meeting for this region, which was held in San Antonio on August 31. Enclosed is a brief report of the two major topics, the marketing strategy to be used last year, and the advertising budgets for the next quarter.

I will be happy to discuss the meeting in further detail at your convience.

lp

🗐 TASK 11

Memo to Sheila Malone
   Re: Quarterly Sales Meeting

I have just returned from attending the quarterly sales meeting for this division, which was held in San Antonio on 8/31. Enclosed is a brief report of the 2 major topics discussed, the marketing strategy to be used next year and the advertising budgets for the next quarter. ¶ I will be happy to discuss the meeting in further detail at your convenience.

H. J. Johnston

▤ TASK 12

Proofread the report below and edit as necessary. Use revision marks to indicate changes needed. This document was typed from the rough draft shown on page 215.

REPORT OF THE QUATERLY SALES MEETING

UNITED STATES DIVISION

August 30, 19--

The quarterly meeting of sales directors for the United States Division was held August 30 at the El Palacio del Rio in San Antonio Texas.

The meeting was called to order by Southwest Regional Sales Director Daniel Buckles. All regional directors were in attendance. All local area directors were not able to attend; 60 percent were in attendance.

Marketing Strategy

The marketing strategy for our primary products was discussed. Participants worked in small groups to develop ideas on possible new strategies for next year. A separate report from Mr. Buckles will outline the strategy decisions that were made.

Advertising Budtet

The advertising budget for each region was presented; this information is presented below.

FOURTH QUARTER ADVERTISING BUDGET

Northeast Region	$1,000,000
Southeast Region	2,500,000
Central Region	3,225,000
Southwest Region	4,110,000
Northwest Region	2,000,000
Total	$11,835,000

📑 TASK 12

REPORT OF THE QUARTERLY SALES MEETING

UNITED STATES DIVISION

August 30, 19--

The quarterly meeting of ~~marketing/~~ sales directors for the United States Division was held August 30 at the El Palacio del Rio in San Antonio Texas.

The meeting was called to order by ~~Marketing/Sales~~ Southwest Regional Sales Director Daniel Buckles. All regional directors were in attendance. All local area directors were not able to attend; 60% were in attendance.

Marketing Strategy

The marketing strategy for our primary products was discussed. Participants worked in small groups to develop ideas on possible new strategies for next year. A separate report from Mr. Buckel's will outline the strategy decisions that were made.

Advertising Budtet

The advertising budget for each region was presented; this information is presented below.

FOURTH QUARTER ADVERTISING BUDGET

Northeast Region	$1,000,000
Southeast Region	2,500,000
Central Region	3,225,000
Southwest Region	4,110,000
Northwest Region	2,000,000
Total	$11,835,000

▤ TASK 13

Proofread the expense claim below and edit as necessary. Use revision marks to indicate changes needed. This document was typed from the handwritten material shown on page 217.

TRAVEL EXPENSE CLAIM

Date	Place Left	Place Arrived	Mileage	Airfare	Hotel	Bkfst.	Lunch	Dinner	Other	Total
8/29	Phoenix	San Antonio		169.00	88.98		5.50	10.25	limosine 5.00	278.73
8/30					88.98	3.25	10.00	12.50		104.73
8/31	San Antonio	Phoenix		169.00		2.85			limosine 5.00	176.85
									airport parking	
									12.00	12.00
TOTALS				338.00	177.96	6.10	15.50	22.75	22.00	572.31

Advance 0.00

Balance 572.31

Signature _____

Date _____

Name H. J. Johnston

Department Sales

▤ TASK 13

Please prepare a Claim for Traveling Expenses for me using this information (be sure to include totals):

8/29

Left Phoenix at 8 a.m., arrived San Antonio 1 p.m.

airfare = $169.—   limousine = $5.—
hotel = $88.98   lunch = $5.50
dinner = $10.25

8/30   (in San Antonio)
hotel = $88.98   breakfast = $3.25
lunch = $10.—   dinner = $12.50

8/31

Left San Antonio at 9 a.m., arrived Phoenix 1 p.m.

airfare = $169.—   breakfast = $2.85
limo = $5.—   airport parking = $12.—

H. J. Johnson
S.S. # 446-00-2002

▤ TASK 14

Proofread the memorandum below and edit as necessary. Use revision marks to indicate changes needed. This document was typed from taped dictation.

MEMORANDUM

TO: All Employees

FROM: Luis Martinez, Accounting Director

DATE;   September 2, 19--

SUBJECT: Profits for Past Fiscal year

We have completed our allocation of income for the past physical year. As shown in the chart below, approximately ⅓ was used for additional employee benefits, ¼ for plant improvements, ¼ for future use, and ⅙ for dividends to stockholders.

ALLOCATION OF INCOME

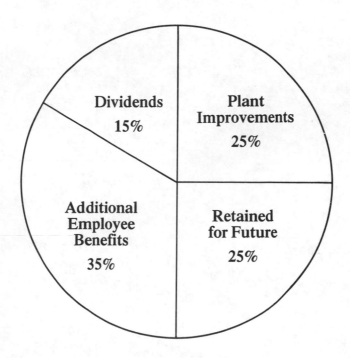

▤ TASK 15

Proofread the memorandum below and edit as necessary. Use revision marks to indicate changes needed. This document was typed from the rough draft shown on page 221. This memorandum is based on information in the next exercise. Refer to the material in task 16 for content accuracy.

MEMORANDUM

TO: Sheila Malone, Administrative Vice President

FROM: Ray Leone, Production Director

DATE: September 2, 19--

SUBJECT: Monthly Production Report

Enclosed is the production report for August. As shown in the report, a majority of the units produced were of Product B.

I will be glad to discuss our production plans with you at anytime.

fp

▤ TASK 15

MEMORANDUM

TO: Sheila Malone, Administrative Vice President
FROM: Ray L~~i~~e̶one, Production Director
SUBJECT: Monthly Production Report
DATE: September 2, 19--

Enclosed ~~please find~~ ᵢₛ the production report for ~~September~~ August. As shown in the report, a majority of the units produced were of Product B.

I will be glad to discuss our production plans with you at anytime.

fp

📑 TASK 16

Proofread the production report below and edit as necessary. Use revision marks to indicate changes needed. This document was typed from taped dictation. Assume that the figures given in the paragraph are correct.

PRODUCTION REPORT

August, 19--

During the month of August, 19--, we used 10,500 pounds of raw materials to produce our 3 major products.   As shown in the chart below, we produced 4,000 units of Product A, 2,000 units of Product B, and 500 units of Product C.

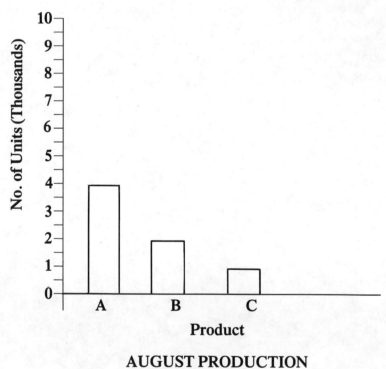

AUGUST PRODUCTION

We have increased our production 20% over this time period last year.

▤ TASK 17

Proofread the memo below and edit as necessary. Use revision marks to indicate changes needed. This document was typed from the rough draft shown on page 225. This memorandum is based on information in the next two exercises. Refer to the material in tasks 19 and 20 for content accuracy.

MEMORANDUM

TO: Sheila Malone, Vice President

FROM: Luis Martinez, Accounting Director

DATE: September 22, 19--

SUBJECT: Financial Statements

Attached are the financial statements for the quarter ending August 30, 19--.

As you will notice on the attached income statement, we had a net income after taxes of $13,200. The balance sheet indicates that we have considerably more in assets than we have in liabilities. We appear to be in good financial position.

If our sales predictions are correct, we should experience an increase in income in the next quarter.

📋 **TASK 17**

MEMORANDUM

TO: Sheila Malone, Vice President

FROM: Luis Martinez, Accounting Director

DATE: September 22, 19--

SUBJECT: Financial Statements

Attached are the financial statements for the quarter ending August 30, 19--.

As you will notice on the attached income statement, we had a net income after taxes of ~~$12,200~~ *($13,200)*. The balance sheet indicates that we have considerably more in assets than we have in liabilities. We appear to be in good financial position.

If our sales predictions are correct, we should experience an increase in income in the next quarter.

📋 TASK 18

Proofread the material below. Use revision marks to indicate changes needed. This document was typed from taped dictation. Assume that the information provided is correct; only the calculations need to be checked.

WORD PROCESSING PRODUCTIVITY REPORT

Employee _____Noel Napier_____   Date _____9/01/--_____

Type of Work	Author's Name/Department	No. of Lines	Time Spent Hours	Minutes
Memo	J. Jones/ Sales	15		20
Letter	L. Chang/Marketing	42	1	10
Memo	P. Ward/Sales	21		45
Report	R. Dobbins/Accounting	358	3	10
Memo	P. Lutz/Legal	18		30
Balance Sheet	M. Piazzi/Accounting	40	1	15
TOTALS		594	6	30

📑 TASK 19

Proofread the balance sheet below and edit as necessary. Use revision marks to indicate changes needed. This document was typed from the handwritten material shown on page 229. Assume that the individual amounts in the original copy are correct, but calculations should be checked.

GREER, INCORPORATED

Balance Sheet

August 31, 19--

Assets

Cash		$67,000
Accounts Receivable	40,000	
Less Allowance for Doubtful Accounts	2,000	38,000
Notes Receivalbe		8,500
Inventories		95,000
Equipment	80,500	
Less Depreciation	10,800	69,700
Total Assets		$278,200

Liabilities

Accounts Payable	22,000
Notes Payable	10,300
Bonds Payable	25,000
Total Liabilities	57,500

Stockholders' Equity

Common stock, par $10, 15,000 shares issued and outstanding	150,000
Contributed capital in excess of par	60,000
Retained Earrings	10,900
Total Stockholders' Equity	220,900
Total Liabilities + Sockholders' Equity	$278,200

▤ TASK 19

Greer Inc.
Bal. Sheet
8/31/19—

Assets

Cash		$67,000
Accts. Receivable	40,000	
Less Allowance for Doubtful Accts.	2,000	38,000
Notes Receivable		8,500
Inventories		95,000
Equipment	80,500	
Less Depreciation	10,800	69,700
Total Assets		$278,200

Liabilities

Accts Payable	22,000
Notes Payable	10,300
Bonds Payable	25,000
Total Liabilities	$57,300

Stockholders' Equity

Common stock, par $10, 15,000 shares issued and outstanding	150,000
Contributed capital in excess of par	60,000
Retained Earnings	10,900
Total Stockholders' Equity	220,900
Total Liabilities + Stockholders' Equity	$278,200

▤ TASK 20

Proofread the income statement below and edit as necessary. Use revision marks to indicate changes needed. This document was typed from the handwritten material shown on page 231. Assume that the individual amounts on the original copy are correct, but calculations should be checked.

GREER, INCORPORATED

Income Statement

For the Quarter Ended August 31, 19--

Revenues:		
Sales	225,000	
Interest	1,000	
Total Revenues		$226,000
Expenses:		
Cost of Goods Sold	112,000	
Operating Expenses	92,000	
Total Expenses		204,000
Pretax Operating Income:		12,000
Income Taxes ($22,000 x .40)		8,800
Net Income After Taxes		$ 13,200

📇 **TASK 20**

all caps
& centered → [Greer, Incorporated
Income Statement
For the Quarter Ended 8/31/19 --

Revenues:

Sales	225,000	
Interest	1,000	
Total Revenues		$226,000

Expenses:

Cost of Goods Sold	112,000	
Operating Expenses	92,000	
Total Expenses		204,000

Pretax Operating Income:	22,000
Income Taxes ($22,000 x .40)	8,800
Net Income After Taxes	$13,200